T0098068

Two Toms

THOMAS H. JOHNSON & HELEN S. JOHNSON

TWO TOMS

LESSONS FROM A SHOSHONE DOCTOR

The University of Utah Press

Salt Lake City

Copyright © 2011 by The University of Utah Press. All rights reserved.

The Defiance House Man colophon is a registered trademark
of The University of Utah Press. It is based upon a four-foot-tall,
Ancient Puebloan pictograph (late PIII) near Glen Canyon, Utah.

LIBRARY OF CONGRESS CATALOGING-IN-PUBLICATION DATA
Johnson, Thomas Hoevet, 1943-
 Two Toms : lessons from a Shoshone doctor / Thomas H. Johnson and Helen S.
Johnson.
    p. cm.
 Includes index.
 ISBN 978-1-60781-090-2 (paper : alk. paper)
 1. Wesaw, Tom, 1886-1973. 2. Shoshoni Indians—Biography. 3. Indian physicians—
Biography. 4. Indian religious leaders—Biography. 5. Johnson, Thomas Hoevet, 1943-
6. Anthropologists—Wyoming—Biography. 7. Wind River Indian Reservation
(Wyo.)—Biography. 8. Shoshoni Indians—Social life and customs.
9. Intercultural communication—Wyoming—Case studies. 10. Friendship—
Wyoming—Case studies. I. Johnson, Helen S. II. Title.
 E99.S4J64 2010
 978.7004'97457400922—dc22
 [B]
                                                        2010050528

For our daughters Thomasina and Cleo,
who accompanied us to Wyoming's beautiful
Wind River Reservation time after time.

Contents

Figures

Introduction

THE WIND RIVER RESERVATION IS IN WEST-CENTRAL WYOMING. ITS 3,400 square miles stretch from the Wind River Mountain Range on the west to high plains in the east and from the Owl Creek Mountains in the north to a southern boundary just above the city of Lander. Originally, the reservation was even larger. The treaty of 1868 gave the reservation to the Eastern Shoshone. Ten years later, in 1878, an executive order by President Hayes placed the Northern Arapaho on the same reservation. It wasn't until 1938 that the United States compensated the Shoshone for settlement of the Arapaho. Forevermore, the assets of the reservation would be divided in half between the two tribes.

The Eastern Shoshone received little anthropological attention until the late 1930s when Demitri Shimkin, then a graduate student at the University of California–Berkeley, visited the reservation. Shimkin learned the Shoshone language and interviewed many of the older Eastern Shoshone on their history and culture. After World War II he published several important monographs on Shoshone ethnogeography, childhood and development, and the Sun Dance. Other anthropologists, such as Fred Voget, Joseph Jorgensen, and me, built upon Shimkin's work on the Sun Dance. As a graduate student in anthropology under Shimkin at the University of Illinois-Champaign-Urbana, I met the subject of this book, Tom Wesaw, in 1966. Tom was a well-known religious leader and you can read more about him in the Smithsonian's *Handbook of North American Indians*, volume 11. Tom gave me permission to enter the Shoshone Sun Dance that he led that year. As a result, we became friends and Tom gave me his blessing and a Sun Dance whistle.

By the time I knew Tom, the Shoshone Sun Dance had changed from a ceremony that included an emphasis on success in warfare to a more general emphasis on healing. Tom was also a leader in the Native American Church, which had come to Wind River around 1900. My interest in

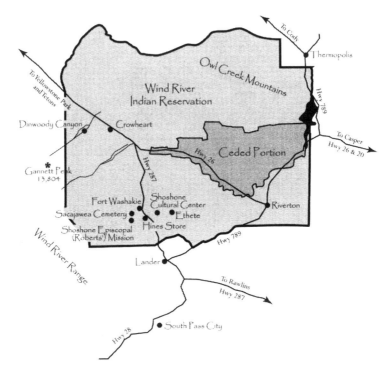

1. Wind River Indian Reservation and surrounding area, located in west-central Wyoming, southeast of Yellowstone and Grand Teton national parks.

Shoshone culture led me to participate in several of their ceremonies; Tom provided entrée to meetings of the Native American Church and sweat lodge ceremonies, which he conducted regularly.

After several visits to the reservation, I returned in 1969 at Tom's request. He knew that my purpose was to study the Shoshone language and whatever he could teach me about Shoshone ways, and he set up a desk and lamp in his house for me to use for my note-taking. All the experiences I include in this book are true and are recorded in field notes written during my stay with him in 1969 and 1970. Some names and characteristics of people both living and dead have been changed to protect privacy. The dialogue in the book is as close as I can reconstruct and is based on field notes. It was during this period that Vida Haukaas came up with the name "Two Toms" because Tom and I were often seen together. Pretty soon, nearly everyone at Wind River referred to us as Two Toms.

I am forever indebted to the openness and generosity given to me by Tom and other members of his extended family. During the 1970s, tensions between American Indians and the dominant society grew. Anthropologists were no longer welcome on some reservations but my friendships among the Shoshone continued during this period. I returned to visit many times over the next decades. I believe that the close relationship that I developed with Tom and his family were partly responsible for this.

Tom was born in 1886. He grew up during a period of much poverty and illness among American Indians. As a middle-aged man in the 1940s, he had tuberculosis and went to a sanatorium in Rapid City, South Dakota, but recovered. The policy of the United States was to assimilate and change the lifeways of Indians. Tom's character and his resistance to imposed change were formed during those years. He took special care of his wife, Helen, who lost her eyesight and died a few years before I knew him. As a doctor and minister to his people, Tom was acutely aware of their suffering and it is that sensitivity that he wanted to pass on to me. This book is a record of some of the experiences I had during the time I spent with him toward the end of his long and generous life. Tom died in 1973.

I
‒

The Pink Phone

Tom Wesaw liked to pay the phone bill in person and in advance. It was his habit to apply extra on the next month's bill because there might be a flurry of collect calls coming in. The employees at the phone company office in Lander came to expect him, tall, spare, and wide-shouldered despite his eighty-some years, natty in a Western shirt and a low-brimmed black Stetson.

His pink, wall-mounted phone rang several times a day. It was his daughter who lived a mile away and did his washing and ironing; it was a close friend; it was a client who depended on Tom for healing. The next call might be from a neighbor on Trout Creek or it might come from a distant part of the reservation like Crowheart Butte, or even beyond Wind River, from relatives in Idaho or Montana.

Tom answered his phone as professionally as any doctor on call. That's what he was, after all—a Shoshone doctor. To the Shoshone, Tom was an "Indian doctor," meaning that he was a doctor in the widest possible sense that Eastern Shoshone people know. Tom was raised with them; he knew their families and had decades of experience. He knew how to pray for them and all his practices—individual healing, peyote meetings, sweat ceremonies, and the Sun Dance—had to do with healing. The term *shaman*, coined by students of comparative religion after Siberian conjurers, was unknown at Wind River. *Medicine man* is the term most non-Indian people would apply to someone like Tom but the term does not bring with it a history of respect. Well into the twentieth century, Indian "medicine men" were thought to be conjurers who practiced a kind of witchcraft.

There was so much prejudice against Indian doctors because European-Americans were trying to correct the quackery and pseudoscience among their own medical practitioners. By the late 1800s scientific medicine had moved away from earlier ideas and practices like bloodletting. The discovery that microbes cause many diseases, the use of antiseptics and immunization and, later, antibiotics, seemed to confirm the superiority of Western medicine. For the American conquerors, it was easier to justify political and social control over the Indian tribes if you could believe that their religion and healing practices were superstitious, false, and primitive. Healing prayer, meditation, singing, and dancing were irrational, the United States government believed, and so the Treaty of 1868 provided for a resident physician at Wind River. As for the Eastern Shoshone, they may never have associated their own religious and healing practices with witchcraft, sorcery, and the medical beliefs of prescientific Europe nor did they accept the Euro-American notion that a hunting-gathering way of life and a political organization based on kinship were inferior to the system of authority imposed on them. In fact, the concept of superstition does not exist among the Shoshone and the word only became part of the English lexicon in the late fourteenth century.

For traditional Shoshone, an Indian doctor like Tom is more important than the physicians at the Indian Health Services clinic. These government doctors spend a limited amount of time with each patient. They prescribe medicines but do not listen much because they do not have the time. They often do not know the Shoshone language and its ways of praying, nor do they honor the power of the eagle. Most physicians do not deal with the spiritual dimension of healing. Mostly, the government doctors come and go, spending two or three years on the reservation with the U.S. Public Health Service to fulfill some obligation to the government.

Tom passed away over thirty years ago but there are still Indian doctors at Wind River. Some specialize in herbal remedies, others in ceremonies. There are men doctors and women doctors. Tom was a one-on-one doctor but he also led ceremonies. When someone called on the phone for doctoring, Tom said, "I'll be there as soon as I can." Making the house call quickly was not easy. Tom no longer drove, which posed problems in continuing his practice. At eighty-three, his eyesight wasn't as good as it used to be. There was no one at home to drive him because he was a widower and had lived alone since the death of his wife several years before. And then there was the plain fact that the Wind River Indian Reservation is huge. It stretches about fifty miles from the granite peaks of the Continental Divide to the sagebrush flats and benches to the east. People usually came to fetch Tom. Sometimes there was quite a delay in getting to the person who needed him.

That changed when I came to stay with Tom in September 1969. Three years before, I had met him at his Sun Dance. He had put it up for all the soldiers fighting in Vietnam. We'd become friends and Tom invited me back to learn about Shoshone healing. His wife had died, he'd explained; it would be nice to have company around. I was to drive him, cook, pump water, and build fires for making sweats in the sweat lodge behind his house. In exchange, he would show me his work. He would be my teacher.

With me in the house and my faithful red Plymouth sedan parked outside under the big cottonwood, Tom had transportation and company. We traveled from one end of the reservation to the other. We visited both Shoshone and Arapaho, for although the treaty of 1868 had given the reservation to the Eastern Shoshone, the United States had placed the Northern Arapaho there, too. Tom had friends among the Arapaho because of his strong connection to the Native American Church. That church came onto the reservation when Tom was a young man. It uses peyote as a sacrament and believes in the unity and brotherhood of all, including whites. Training me, a young white guy not even from Wyoming, was a way of living his beliefs.

When Tom invited me to stay with him, he gave me a small table, chair, and lamp. "It's for you to do your study," he said, knowing that I was an anthropology student. By the light of the lamp he'd given me, sitting at that table, I was to write down what I learned. I was to tell everything I saw and heard. That was my training as an anthropologist and it was my agreement with Tom. If something was not for my ears, I was excluded.

"I'll be there as soon as I can," I can hear him saying into the receiver of his pink, wall-mounted phone. He's looking at me and raising his eyebrows. I nod, a little distracted by a bee flying around the room. It had come in through the front door. The door faced east, just as tipi openings faced east in the old days. And just like those old days, Tom greeted the morning with arms uplifted in prayer. He left his door open any early morning if the day promised to be bright and warm. The windows of his house were small and he preferred the calico curtains to be pushed open. Over the kitchen window grew vines planted by his wife years before, cool and green. We are in early September. Today promises to be a hot one.

"I'll be there," Tom says into the phone. "As soon as I can, Sondra."

The bee zigzags out the front door. Tom's house had two rooms: a kitchen and one big room with a divider that went only waist-high. His old-fashioned, cast-iron bed was against the back wall of the big room. Tom kept his peyote box, eagle-feather fan, and beaded belt in a suitcase under his bed. On the unpainted sheetrock wall facing the bed hung religious pictures—Jesus knocking at the door, Mary, Jesus's sacred heart—and on the opposite wall, family portraits. I used to like to look from Jesus and Mary and the heart to Tom's Uncle Bishop Wesaw in full traditional attire, a hand-colored photo from the 1890s.

My bed was by the front door, across from the pink phone. Like Tom, I kept things under my bed. My suitcase with all my clothes was there. I never unpacked because there was no chest to put the clothes in.

I see Tom hauling his suitcase from under his bed. He takes out his eagle feather fan and his smaller peyote fan made from woodpecker feathers, a bag of cedar needles, and a plain white china saucer.

Outside, a gust of hot wind sends a sprinkling of yellow leaves from the cottonwood onto the red hood of my car. The plastic seats are hot to the touch. I back the car and turn it around. That was the only way to head out his single-track lane. To open the gate at the end of Tom's lane, you had to get out of the car and remove the loop of wire that held the makeshift gate to the fence post. The gate didn't swing wide, so you had to pick up the gatepost and walk it far enough over for the car to pass. I had done this many times before at my grandparents' place in Iowa. Just like in Iowa, where grandpa's pasture was rented out, it was important to remember to close the gate after your car reached the other side because Tom also rented out his pasture.

"Cattle," he says out the car window as we drive past the cows. "How I hate their bellering. They keep coming up to the house. They make guidup all the time on my vines."

"Guidup?" I ask, turning onto the paved road. *Guidup* was a Shoshone word I had not heard yet.

"Cow guidup. Cow pies," Tom says with exasperation. "The first turn up Trout Creek leads up to Sondra's place."

Sondra's place turned out to be a log house quite a distance away from the road. A young Shoshone woman in jeans and a T-shirt stood at the door. Her hair fell about her shoulders. With a glance, I asked Tom, *Should I stay in the car?*

He shook his head. "You come with me," he said.

It didn't seem polite to look at the woman's face. It was puffy from crying. So I followed her and Tom through the front door and into the front room. It wasn't until we were inside the house and the three of us were sitting that Tom spoke another word. He asked, "Sondra, how's your mom and dad?"

She didn't answer. Her hand was gripping the side of her chair so tightly that her knuckles were white. I looked away from her hand to the floor. Over the linoleum lay a rag rug and over that a sheepskin. My gaze skipped around the room to a round table for eating covered with an oil-cloth, an old floor lamp, and, on the wall, a calendar from a lumber yard. This month's picture was the Grand Tetons.

I looked back at Sondra's hand. Tom had taken it in his. "Now everything's going to be all right," Tom told her.

"Mom's okay but I had some *really* bad dreams last night and I want you to pray for me," she said.

I had heard about the importance of dreams for Native people. Young people will seek a vision after fasting for a long period of time in order to receive a dream. The dream will give them a direction in life. The Shoshone people told me about how certain doctors had received their power by sleeping near a rock-carving in a certain canyon on the reservation. A dream came to the doctors that they were to heal others. I had also heard how dreams could portend disaster, even death. Dreams were not to be taken lightly.

Instead of asking questions or probing into Sondra's inner life as a psychiatrist would, Tom put the china saucer he had brought with him on the nearby table. His power had come from his Uncle Bishop Wesaw who had given him his Sundance whistle and an eagle feather fan. The objects were not powerful in themselves; they represented the higher power in the universe that the Shoshone call *Dam Apë*, Our Father. By giving Tom the whistle and fan, his uncle had transferred some of his power.

Tom took the bag of cedar needles out of his peyote box and placed them in the saucer. He struck a match and held the flame to the needles. Their smolder sent the sharp sweet fragrance of cedar into the room. Tom took up his eagle feather fan in one hand and his peyote fan in the other, using them to slowly guide the cedar smoke toward Sondra.

She lowered her head and closed her eyes.

"*Nuh nanaishuntai*," Tom said. "I am going to pray now. *Dam Apë* have pity on your child. Make her feel better."

He was brushing Sondra with the feather fans, beginning on one side and moving up over her arm, over her shoulder, then her head, and down the other side of her body. Tom's brushing was as light as a feather, you might say.

Sondra sat still, letting him brush her. Her breath came short and shallow and her lips trembled. She was trying to smother her sobs. I couldn't tell if the brushing was of any comfort.

Tom put down his fans and waited. In a few moments, he held out his hand to her. She took it and they sat there, Tom waiting, Sondra choking back feelings. There was no sense of urgency. This house call was going to take as long as it was going to take.

"Take away her fears," Tom prayed. "Make her feel at peace."

A line of tears trailed down her cheeks. Her hand brushed at them. Sondra was taking deeper, ragged breaths now.

"Our elder brother Jesus take away her bad dreams," Tom prayed. His exact words were *som bavi Jesus*. Bavi is the term for a respected older brother, Brother Jesus.

Sondra straightened up in her chair. She took a deep breath through her nose, then breathed out. She swallowed hard and opened her eyes.

Tom laid the fans beside the china dish. He placed his hands over Sondra's and gave a gentle squeeze.

She looked up at him and smiled.

No more was said. We left Sondra sitting in her chair. In the car on the way home I said, "She seemed to feel much better."

"She's a good woman who tries to lead a good life," was Tom's reply. "I know Sondra and her family. Her stepmother and she don't get along. Her stepmother is very jealous of her in a bad way and her *baha*, her father's older sister, takes the stepmother's side. I know—my stepmother was a bad one, too. I left home as soon as I possibly could. My mom died in childbirth with me. My dad remarried some years later. When I was about fifteen, I could leave home. I had a good horse and I traveled to Idaho to my relatives up there. I worked over there, you know. Then I came back and married Helen Hill. When our George was born, I promised myself my kids' life would be happier than mine had been. About that time, I started learning to be a doctor. I assisted in peyote meetings and danced in Sun Dances. I knew that white doctors could help people in some ways but they couldn't help people in other ways."

"Would Sondra have felt comfortable going to a white man's doctor for the bad dreams she was having?" I asked.

"No," Tom said. "White men's medicine doesn't have what it takes to help Indians. It has pills and shots and blood pressure. I use aspirin with some people and some liniments. My aspirin and their pills and shots couldn't help Sondra. Just my blessing and my prayers were what she needed."

"Do you ever use Indian herbs?" I asked.

"I always keep a bag of Indian perfume in my pocket," he said. "It's an herb I get from Oklahoma, very sweet smelling. If someone feels sick to their stomach, I put it up to their nose, sort of like sweet sage. Peyote is an herb and I like that for certain things but usually give it to people only as a tea, except that we use regular ground peyote in ceremonies."

Many kitchen windowsills on the reservation held flower pots of peyote cacti. I saw peyote buttons the diameter of a soup bowl. Some Shoshone went down to the peyote gardens near Laredo, Texas. To get the peyote back home, they hid it in blankets and suitcases and any other place you can think of. In those days there was always the threat of legal action if you were caught using or transporting peyote, even though for members of the Native American Church peyote is a sacrament.

"My uncle taught me how to pray," Tom said. "His uncle before him taught him. These are old ways that have worked for many years for Indian people long before the white man came. Whites trust in pills. I always say prayers, too, and it is those prayers that heal. *Dam Apë* heals and Jesus Our Elder Brother was a great healer. You could be a healer, too, Johnson, but right now you don't believe strong enough. You have just a little belief. Maybe when you're an old man like me you'll have strong enough belief. Another thing, it's better if you know the people maybe for your whole life to help them. I know and help whole families, know them for many years. They know me as the man I am and I know them. It's something that grows on you over time—maybe twenty, thirty years. I started leading Sun Dances many years ago. But you can learn by sticking by me, Johnson, if you really want to, and you can learn that Shoshone language and songs, too."

"How does it feel when you're brushed with those eagle fans?" I asked.

"The eagle has the strength to fly higher than any other bird, closer to God than any animal. The fan is like an eagle swooping down and touching

2. Tom Wesaw in front of his house, 1967. He wears a bolo tie with the peyote semicircle design. All photos by Thomas H. Johnson.

you. You feel different; you feel the eagle's power. It came from God. I can't tell you anything more. You just know that God's power is there."

We drove in silence for a few minutes and I imagined what it would be like to be so close to a swooping eagle that I could feel its brushing wings and the wave of air behind. It could feel like an electric shock or send shivers up your spine. The eagle is a messenger from God.

The clinic at Fort Washakie and the hospital in nearby Lander were beginning to let these Indian doctors come in and pray for patients, just the same as they did with priests or ministers. As with priests and ministers, doctoring was not about money. Still, I wondered if Tom expected some kind of compensation, either monetary or in-kind.

I didn't have long to wait to find out. The next day, Tom was finishing his coffee and I was pouring hot water from the kettle on the stove into the dishpan to do the morning dishes when we heard a car drive up the lane. I hadn't heard the pink phone ring that morning, and Tom was not in the mood to see anybody; but if you are a doctor you have to put up with people showing up at your door at any time.

Tom grumbled, "Go see who it is, Johnson."

I glanced out the window. A man had parked his red pickup next to my car under the cottonwood. He was getting out and taking something out of the back of his truck: a large package wrapped in white butcher paper.

"I don't know who it is," I said. "Do you know?"

Tom got up to have a look. "That's Sondra's older brother, Gene."

Gene had evidently been to the house before because he walked right in. "How's Sondra?" Tom asked.

"Feeling much better today," Gene told him. "She went down to Rocky Mountain Hall to play the hand game last night. I'm glad you came by to doctor her."

"*Deeveejee zhant*," Tom said. I knew that meant literally "very good," but it also meant that he was glad to hear the news about Gene's sister.

"*Deeveejee zhant*," I repeated under my breath. I was glad, too.

Gene cleared his throat. "I brought you some fresh elk meat. I want you to have a good supper tonight."

Elk. So that was what was in the package. I'd never eaten elk, but I had been told that elk meat is very tasty, far better than beef. Since I'd been on the reservation I had tried all kinds of new foods. Bear is rich and should be eaten with mashed potatoes served with a big ladle of gravy. Antelope

is also rich, but because antelope eat so much sagebrush, their meat is fla-
vored with sage. The same goes for the juicy sage chickens that live in the
foothill meadows around the reservation.

Tom's mood had changed for the better. He obviously liked it when
people brought gifts of meat for what he had done for them. It must be the
Shoshone way to return a kindness with another kindness, I decided. It
must be the best way for Shoshone people to behave toward each other.

That afternoon I cut one of the elk steaks into cubes for a stew. Into
the hot Dutch oven they went and sizzled in bacon grease with some
onions until brown. I threw in two large handfuls of carrots, some potatoes
and a stalk of celery, and a little salt. There was a hand-pump in the kitchen
that drew water from the well just outside. The water came out ice-cold
and sweet. A quart of it went into the stew pot.

Tom came into the kitchen. He looked at me and nodded. "You're
darn good cook. That elk meat came just at the right time."

Truth was, I wasn't much of a cook at all. I'd learned to make a decent
gravy and that was about it.

The next day I made an elk pot roast. The day after that, ground elk
became hamburgers. Tom appreciated it all. I had never tasted any kind of
meat that was as good as that elk.

Now, all that was left was the elk's liver. In the butcher paper, it was
heavy like a rock. Should I slice it and fry it with onions and bacon? I
wondered. How about pouring a can or two of tomato sauce over the liver
and baking it in the oven. My mother back in Iowa fixed liver those ways.
I knew one thing for certain about liver: never overcook it. That would be
my guide.

I took the liver out of its wrapping. It lay on the kitchen table, huge.
There must have been at least five pounds of elk liver with pea-green bile
beginning to rise to the surface.

Bile couldn't add much to the good taste of liver and certainly it was
an impurity, I said to myself. I was glad it had risen to the surface. I washed
it off and dried it with a paper towel.

Tom and I were due at the house of a peyote brother of his later that
evening. We three were driving into town to catch the John Wayne film
Rio Bravo at the Grand Theatre. That movie came back every couple of
years, Tom told me. He wouldn't mind seeing it for the third time. We had
to eat quickly.

The liver sliced up easily. Half I put back in the butcher paper for another meal. The rest I floured and salted and fried up with some onions. Along with some boiled potatoes, it would make a good supper. It certainly smelled savory.

"What is that?" Tom growled from the other room.

He must not like liver, I thought. He could have told me. "Liver and onions and boiled potatoes and my famous gravy," I called back.

Tom's footfall was heavy and quick. "That liver's spoiled," he shouted. "We can't eat that tonight. I'm going on a date with my girlfriend. I don't want to be sick."

I turned off the stove, swallowing back the realization that the bile I had washed off meant that the liver I had sliced, floured, and fried was spoiled.

"You didn't know," he said softly. "Let's go for hamburgers tonight. Doreen would like a trip to the Dairy Queen for hamburgers."

"Who's Doreen? I thought we were taking Luke Walters to the movies."

Tom stood up a little taller. "Luke is going. So's his daughter, Doreen."

I stared at Tom in blank amazement. I had already met Luke Walters—he looked to be about fifty. His daughter would have to be about half that age. That would make her more like my age and fifty or sixty years younger than Tom.

"She's my DATE!" he laughed. "I'm thinking of getting married again."

Hat and Shoes

"Doreen is a honey," Tom said the next morning.

I gave the scrambled eggs in the pan a rake with a wooden spoon. Last night I had chauffeured Tom and Doreen and her dad. Doreen seemed nice enough. She was young and pretty, with long, dark hair. She hadn't said much but her dad and I had been right there the whole time. I kept thinking Doreen looked as if she were doing her father a favor by sitting next to Tom.

I knew I could be wrong about that. In the old days, it wasn't all that unusual for an older Shoshone man to marry a much younger woman. The same went for older women and younger men. Some Shoshone men had more than one wife; usually, it was two sisters but most Shoshone lived in monogamous unions. Traditionally, people who married simply agreed to live together and help each other with a practical bond that became stronger over time. Older people who were widowed needed a younger person to help with all the work of hunting, dressing hides, and gathering plant foods. People lived in extended three- or four-generation families. This kind of arrangement made good sense then, and I knew of several families that still lived this way. It wasn't until about 1900 that the U.S. government's reservation agent began to require all people living in Shoshone-style marriages to go through the formal process of getting married. It was kind of beside the point, as most of the Shoshone had been married for many years, but it was a way of enforcing the government's attempt to control plural marriages and change the culture. Land needed to be probated and passed on to heirs, giving the government another reason to require legal marriage, rather than common-law marriage. All this formality came with the adoption of American methods of recognizing estates in the early 1900s.

Tom chuckled. "*Waipe Suguaint*—Wants-A-Woman. That's your name now. You're stuck with it."

I had to bite my cheeks to keep myself from laughing. If I laughed I'd never get rid of that nickname for as long as I was around Tom.

"Now I teach you more Shoshone words," Tom said. I glanced at him but he didn't spot that because he was busy filling his mug with coffee. He was smiling to himself. He poured some milk into the coffee, still smiling, and added sugar. He stirred his mug, his eyes crinkled into silent laughter. "You good man, *Waipe Suguaint*," Tom said.

"Thanks," I shrugged.

"We want you stay around here. We want you to find some cute *naibe*—Indian girl—and have lots of *nuwu direpere*—Shoshone kids."

This was a joke meant to be a compliment. I scooped the eggs onto two plates, one for me, one for him, and handed Tom his. At table, Tom pointed his index finger at me. "*Waipe Suguaint*," he said, "I'm going to tell you. You need many good words, as much help as I can give you. Yes, many good words are needed." He nodded, agreeing with himself, then ate a quick forkful of scrambled eggs. There was no need to ask *Good words for what?* after he'd been calling me Wants-A-Woman.

Tom smiled. "I'm going to tell you many good words, words you use to get a Shoshone woman."

I was about to try to change the subject but just then it occurred to me to call Tom's bluff. My pen and the notebook where I wrote down Shoshone phrases to memorize were on the kitchen table. I picked up the pen, paged through the notebook to a blank page, and waited for the language lesson.

Tom shrugged. "I'll tell you the words you need to know to sweet talk your Shoshone girlfriends after we get back from Fort Washakie," he said, getting up. "I need to call on the lease clerk over there. Let's ghost."

That joke was safe to laugh aloud at but when I did, Tom looked at me, surprised.

"I'm almost a ghost because I'm so old," he said. "Shoshone say their word for ghost is *zho*, the same word as for great-grandpa and that's what I am, a great-grandpa. Someday soon I may be a ghost, too."

With Doreen around, it didn't seem to me that Tom was thinking about ghosting anytime soon. Now he took his black Stetson from the peg on the wall near the door. That hat was kind of a trademark with him. You could tell it was Tom Wesaw from a long way away by the shape of that hat. Nobody else had one exactly like it, with its low crown and wide brim.

Fort Washakie isn't really a town. It's a BIA or Bureau of Indian Affairs post that started life as an army fort. In those days, a couple dozen white frame houses lined the streets, most of them homes of the employ-ees of the local branch of the Bureau of Indian Affairs. Over there was the tribal health clinic, and a woman getting into her car in the parking lot. Next to it was the big white frame Victorian house euphemistically called "The Big Teepee"—the house that used to be reserved for the agent, who represented the United States government. Next to the clinic was a row of low stone buildings that once had been army barracks. A large cottonwood shaded the lawn in front of all these buildings. The lawn was always kept green, just about the only green lawn on the reservation. Across the park-ing lot, an old stone building—the Bureau of Indian Affairs Agency office.

We parked next to the agency and I followed Tom up the stairs and into the lobby of the building. Several employees greeted him but Tom walked right up to a middle-aged white woman with a bouffant hairdo and many rings on her fingers. He didn't doff his Stetson.

"How are you today, Tom?" the woman asked.

Tom scratched his ear. "You got any lease money for me yet?"

I thought about the cows making pies in Tom's yard. An irrigation ditch went through his land. For a while, as a young man, Tom raised wheat. The agency operated a flour mill in those days and Tom worked there as a miller. When Tom gave up farming, one of his sons raised barley on the allotment. He got good prices for it during World War II, but as prices fell so did his interest in farming. As near as I could tell, the land had been in alfalfa for years and was leased out. Tom rented out his pas-ture, but the land did not belong to him. It was an allotment, a loan of land from the government to each Shoshone. The Dawes Severalty or Allot-ment Act of 1887 was enacted with the idea of getting the Indians to start farming, but ownership in the white man's sense was not part of the arrangement. The land was Tom's to farm or to sublet, as he chose, but the actual owner of the land was still the federal government.

The lease clerk retrieved a file from a drawer. She took a moment to flip through it. "Clayton only paid half of his rent this early," she said. "He promised to pay the rest at the end of this month when he sells a couple more cows."

I saw how Tom's expression changed. He frowned and said nothing. The lease clerk had made the arrangement for a deferred payment with the renter without telling Tom. Tom had plans to buy needed things, and now he was only going to get half the amount owed him.

Tom said, "I need to pay some bills."

The lease clerk smiled at him. "All I can do is give you the half that he paid me. It's forty dollars for this month."

Tom took the money and we left. Outside it was hot and getting hotter. The sprinklers had been turned on. We had to walk through them to get to the car.

"That lease clerk's always pulling things like that," Tom said. "She knows Clayton and likes him. Clayton's *taivo*—white—and I'm an Indian."

"Why don't you collect the lease money yourself?" I asked.

"The bureau does all of that. The bureau collects the money from the renters, then they shell it out to the Indians. The government really owns the land and we just get to sit on it. Some still graze a few cattle, but I'm too old."

"I thought this was your land," I said. "You got it in a treaty."

"Long time ago when I was a boy, the government wanted to teach us to farm so they gave us all some land," Tom said. "They said the land really wasn't ours because we were still wards of the government. We were like children who couldn't pay their bills yet, the government said."

"But that was so long ago."

"You bet," Tom said. "It's high time the government gave that land to us so we can collect rent if we rent out our land, just like anybody else."

We drove away from the Fort with the windows rolled down, the warm September wind in our faces. It was fifteen miles to Lander, the county seat. Tom said nothing at all during those fifteen miles. That gave me time to think. I would have asked to see the head of land operations at the BIA and demanded an explanation, I told myself. Instead, Tom had said nothing, but then he had about eighty more years of experience with the Bureau of Indian Affairs than I did. The allotment system never accomplished what its framers had hoped, because congressmen in Washington didn't understand Indians. One of the army officers who came in to take over the corrupt administration of the Wind River Reservation in the 1890s protested the allotment system. Captain Patrick Henry Ray tried to organize opposition to the allotments, arguing that Indian people lived communally and weren't used to building up capital. It made sense but Ray's voice was a lone one in 1892 in Wyoming. He was run off the reservation by organized local opposition, and the Wyoming state legislature petitioned Congress to have him removed. The U.S. Army reassigned him to Alaska.

Each Indian family was given so much land to work, with the idea of turning them into farmers and ranchers on the American model of the family-run farm. The land would be "loaned" to the Indians until they could make it into a profitable operation, supposedly twenty-five years. So, while Indians didn't have to pay taxes on allotted land, they also had to pass all control over the proceeds to the BIA. A little later, the government finally decided that Indians were in such bad financial straits that they could sell their right to the allotment after twenty-five years. Starting from scratch and without enough capital to build a farming or ranching operation, many Indian families did sell.

Once the land passed from Indian allotment to white ownership, the federal government was no longer involved. Thousands of acres of reservation land that could have been used for tribal grazing lands or managed by families passed from Indian allotment to white ownership, creating even more grinding poverty for the Shoshone. If I, as an American homesteader, had been dealt that hand of cards, having little capital to create a profitable farming operation, I would have sold out for what I could get, too. As I later found out, those whites who had money in Fremont County eventually bought out the small allotments with help from BIA clerks who had ties to local realtors. Again, Mr. Indian was screwed.

Tom and I were coming into Lander now. There on the left was the Dairy Queen where we'd eaten with Doreen and her father the night before. I slowed to forty-five, then thirty-five, then to twenty-five, passing the Wagon Wheel Motel on one side of Main Street and the Maverick Motel on the other. We drove by the Buckhorn Saddle Shop and the Mint Bar.

"Park in this block," Tom said. "We're going to go see my nephew, Joe."

I eased into a space across the street from a low building with the sign of a cowboy swinging a lariat. The sign said Joe's Place, Western Clothing for Men.

Tom didn't wait for me. Half a moment later, he was pulling open the store's door. The bell jingled. It jingled when I opened the door, too.

A tall young man was holding out his hand to Tom. His hair was black and straight, combed back from a handsome bronze face. Well-pressed tan trousers, a dark blue shirt with pearlized snaps, a tan sport coat with peaked Western yokes, and a bolo tie with a big turquoise inset—he dressed like some of the well-to-do ranchers I'd seen in town.

"This is my nephew," Tom told me.

Joe and I exchanged nods. He must have known that I was the guy who the Shoshone called *duiwichee–taivo*, young white man. I was the one who was driving Tom around and staying with him.

"Tom, I was just waitin' for you to come in," Joe said. He motioned to a stack of black Stetsons on a shelf behind the cash register. The hats were just like the one Tom was wearing.

On both sides of the store were shelves full of folded shirts and pants. In the middle of the store there were racks of new, stiff, denim jackets and fancy belts with flowers and arrows and cattle brands tooled into the leather. There were stacks of fancy neckerchiefs and everyday calico bandanas, your choice of blue or red. Tom ignored it all. He went behind the cash register to the Stetsons.

"Tom's my uncle because my mother is like a sister to him in the Indian way," Joe said, looking my way. "My grandmother and Tom's mother were sisters."

"How is your mom?" Tom asked. He had taken off his own hat and was trying on a new one. It was exactly like the old one.

"Mom moved off the old home place at Fort Washakie a couple years ago. There was just too much work to do so we leased out the ranch and the house. She's living with my brother in town now."

It crossed my mind that this successful business family might also have to get their rent money for the ranch through the clerk at Fort Washakie. It would depend on whether Joe's mother's place at the Fort was allotted land like Tom's or deeded land. If it was deeded, the family owned it outright and could manage it themselves.

Tom took off the new Stetson and put on his own again. He turned to Joe. "All of your brothers and sisters have left the reservation now."

Joe nodded.

"Maybe we'll go visit with your mom," Tom said. He put the new hat back on the shelf. "I haven't seen Felicia for long time. I sure like that new hat. I'll be back some other time for it, you can sure bet on that."

I stepped aside to let Tom by. His quick step I put to a change of plan that involved a visit to Joe's mother in her new home.

I started to follow him out.

"Johnson, you wait for me back at the car," he called over his shoulder. He was moving with purpose and I found myself smiling, wondering what he was up to.

"Well, I call that kind of interesting," Joe said, beginning to straighten a display of bolo ties. "I better call Mom and tell her to expect a visit."

It turned out that Tom had gone next door to Tradehome Shoes. He bought a pair for Doreen, black patent leather heels, the kind of thing she was unlikely to wear around the ranch. Tom put the box of shoes in the back seat of the car.

We didn't go to Joe's mom's directly. Tom said he could use an ice cream so we walked to the end of the block. It was past lunch rush at the NuWay Café and there were plenty of empty booths. We each ordered a dish of ice cream and a cup of coffee and Tom told me that Joe's mom, Felicia, was "a real lady, someone you'd want to take on a date. Her grandfather was a Mormon missionary who married a Shoshone woman back in the early days."

"Are you going to ask her out?" I asked.

"I can't. She's my sister. You'd call her my cousin but, to me, she's my sister. But you could ask her out," he laughed.

It turned out that Felicia lived in a newer subdivision up on a hill overlooking Lander. In place of the cyclone fences and dry, unwatered front yards of the older part of town below, up here there were manicured lawns and rose bushes. Tom, who was repeating to me that his mother and Felicia's were sisters, and in the Indian way, mother's sisters were called "mother" and their children, "sister" or "brother," was smiling. He stopped himself in mid-sentence. "Well, look at this place!"

I hadn't even taken the key out of the ignition when Felicia opened the door. Her smiling, light brown face was set off by snow-white hair and a string of pearls around her neck. She wore the kind of dress my grandmother would put on for church. I didn't know if she dressed up just for us but if she had, that, too, was something my grandmother would have done.

We followed her into the house. The entryway smelled of lemon Pledge. Silky, sheer curtains on the tall windows muted the sun. Felicia—still smiling, telling Tom how nice it was to see him, saying how nice it was to meet me—led us onto the wall-to-wall shag carpet and past a glass-fronted china closet to a sofa upholstered in blue with pink roses. A grandfather clock ticked away the time in the corner, and a cut-glass vase of garden roses sat on the coffee-table.

"Tom, I haven't seen you in years," she said, motioning to us to sit down. "How are you and your family?"

They visited a while like that, talking over the past, catching up on news. My eyes wandered to the family photos on the wall. I wasn't at all surprised that some were the same as I saw every day at Tom's house, like the portrait of their grandfather Enos in his reservation hat and another of five of his daughters grouped around several of their children taken in the 1870s.

"Yeah, Johnson, those pictures bring back memories," Tom said.

"Remember Grampa's white horse?" Felicia asked.

"Sure I do," Tom said. "My young *taivo* friend here, Tom Johnson, he wants to hear something about the way your dad lost his life so many years ago because he study the stories of history of our tribe, and your dad was important chief way back."

"That's so true," Felicia said. "My dad was George Terry, son of Joshua Terry and a Shoshone woman, Julia Greasewood. You know, the Shoshones trusted dad so much they made him chairman of the council. I guess that's the same thing as chief, because old Chief Washakie had died and the tribe asked him to step in. My dad was about to go back to Washington to find out from the BIA why the Shoshones never got their check after giving away so much land to the government. The government wanted to open up all the reservations to homesteaders about 1900. They took the entire reservation north of Big Wind River. I was just a little girl then, but I heard the story many times later on. You know I was just seven when Papa was murdered. Tom, you're older than me. You must remember that."

Tom closed his eyes, remembering. "I was a young man living in Idaho when it happened, but I heard a story about it—everybody talked about it when I came back. But you tell what you know first."

"It was a dark night in the middle of winter," Felicia said. I found myself thinking that she had undoubtedly told this story many times. "Papa had gone out to the barn before bed to check on the horses. Suddenly, all the hay in the barn caught fire and soon the entire barn was ablaze. The horses whinnied and tossed their heads. They were so scared they tried to bolt, but some couldn't get out. Momma and us kids quickly got on our clothes, but Momma said we should stay in the house. She went out, but couldn't get near the barn because it was all on fire. We didn't know what happened to Papa, but we knew he was out there, somewhere."

"There was no fire department in those days," Tom said.

"And we lived a mile from the Fort. Neighbors began to come in from all directions to see if we were all right. Everybody asked about Papa, but the fire was so hot no one dared go into the barn. We feared he was dead, burned in the fire. Next day, after the barn was in ashes, someone found Papa's body behind the barn, near the creek. His head had a terrible gash on one side and a tomahawk, one of those dime-store tomahawks, not anything the Shoshone or Arapaho would have ever had, lay all bloody nearby. Somebody had wanted to kill Papa and they started a fire in the barn to get him outside at night."

"Nobody ever found out who killed him," Tom said.

"No," Felicia agreed, "but everybody knew Papa was about to go back to Washington to find out why we never got our money for all that land we gave back to the government. Somebody wanted to stop him, and everybody said that the tomahawk was a way of pinning the blame on some Indians. But why would an Indian have wanted to kill Papa? He was doing what the tribe wanted. He had some information that he wanted to tell the government in Washington, but couldn't without going there, and somebody had to stop him. Inspectors came out to try to find out who killed my papa, but the crime was never solved, nobody was ever brought to trial."

"No Shoshone Indian killed him," Tom said. "I think it was a hired killer and that person wanted to lay the blame on the Indians." He looked over at me. "I was about your age, Johnson. There was one Indian who suddenly got favors from the government. He got to lease some coal mines on the reservation, even though the tribal council didn't want one Indian to get more money than others."

Felicia nodded. "People said that they knew who had the motive to kill Papa, but the superintendent protected that person. He might have hired some killer to do the deed. There are always people like that but no one knows for sure and probably we'll never know. Anyway, I never heard if we got our money or not, but we did lose our land, and just about that time, homesteaders came onto the reservation and started the town of Riverton. We Shoshones had given part of our reservation to the Arapahos, and now the government forced us to give a big chunk of it to the homesteaders. I can't tell you how mad my folks, my mother's people were. Dad's folks were all in Utah. He was a half-breed but always took the side of the Indians."

Back on the highway on the way home, Tom asked me to stop at Doreen's. He wanted to give the shoes to her right now, he said.

This was one of those times I stayed in the car; Tom didn't invite me to come in. I watched him walk to the door. It would have been hard not to notice how youthful Tom suddenly seemed. Then a woman opened the door. It wasn't Doreen.

That must be his future mother-in-law, I thought, not believing that at all, and I leaned out the open window to look up at the clear blue sky. I expected to wait a good long time.

The wait lasted only a few minutes. I heard the door open and Tom's voice saying, "See you soon, honey."

Tom had a grin on his face.

3

Peyote

A LIST OF PLACES WE SAW DOREEN, FROM MY FIELDNOTES:

- Dance at Rocky Mountain Hall: Tom decides to sit on the bleachers with Doreen and her father. Later, Doreen participates in the women's dance. Tom there to watch.
- Shopping trip to Lander for another pair of high heels: Tom doesn't find any that are patent leather so buys nothing and doesn't see Doreen.
- Funeral Feast at Rocky Mountain Hall: Doreen stands in a food line and doesn't go out of her way to greet Tom.
- Coffee at the NuWay Café in Lander: Doreen walks in and sits down in a booth across the aisle from us and says "Hi, Two Toms." It's what everyone is calling us now. It takes Tom two weeks to drop the Wants-A-Woman name for me, although he continues to call me that every once in a while. He calls me mostly by my last name.

Off and on like that for the next weeks it went with Doreen. Tom never talked about her. He was busy. Every couple of days, we made a trip into Lander to buy things or have pie and coffee or visit old-timers whose memories went back as far as Tom's. I took Tom on professional calls at the hospital. He continued to minister to people on the reservation, as well. He seemed happy. Maybe Doreen was a temporary flirtation. Maybe Tom had lost interest.

The leaves on the cottonwoods had begun to turn a bright yellow and the nights to grow crisp as October arrived. One morning, I blinked at the thin, gray light coming through the red calico curtains above my bed, punched up my pillow, and turned onto my other side. My nose was cold.

The rest of me could have used an extra blanket. Outside, I knew, frost glittered on the grass.

The pink phone rang.

I got out of bed to answer it. The floor was cold. I hopped gingerly over to the phone. "Hello," I said, standing on the sides of my feet because of the cold floor. "This is Tom Wesaw's place."

"You're not Tom," a woman's voice answered.

I held out the phone to Tom. He took it from me and began talking in rapid Shoshone.

I pulled on thick wool socks, listening hard to what he was saying in Shoshone, trying to pick out every other word. There was *baha* (a father's sister), *dabe* (today), and something that sounded an awful lot like *Idaho*. I pulled on my jeans and threw on a heavy flannel shirt. Tom was talking fast. If, someday, I spoke Shoshone half as well as Tom spoke English, I thought for the hundredth time, I'd be happy.

Tom hung up the phone. "Can you take us to Idaho today, Johnson? My niece is about to have a baby. She needs the blessings of a peyote meeting real soon. Her grandmother is my sister."

Father's sister's daughter, *today*, *Idaho*: I felt pretty pleased with myself.

"Where in Idaho?" I asked.

"Fort Hall."

"That's probably five or six hours away?"

Tom gave a nod. "My niece's husband is up at the Crow Reservation in Montana breaking horses. Her brother is about to go to Vietnam. She really needs my help and we can all use your help, too."

"Sure," I said. "We'll drive over right away."

I wanted to help, plus I had not yet been to Fort Hall and had not met Tom's relatives who lived there. Wind River and Fort Hall people are closely related but had been split into two groups long before the treaty of 1868. Chief Washakie's band got the bigger reservation in Wyoming and Chief Pocatello a smaller one around old Fort Hall, first a Hudson's Bay trading post and then an American one. When the railroad came through, Pocatello had to cede the land the government needed for a small amount of money and the town that sprang up was named after him.

Tom and I had barely time to eat a bowl of cereal. We had a long drive ahead of us and the sooner we started, the better. Tom's peyote meeting would begin the next evening, Saturday, and last until daybreak Sunday. By

3. Tom Wesaw on our trip to Fort Hall, Idaho, October 1969.

the time I'd thrown a few clothes in my backpack and grabbed my sleeping bag, Tom was already packed. He was waiting with his box of peyote fans and his peyote staff, and was wearing a new bolo tie I hadn't seen.

Outside, our breath hung in the air. The vines next to the house were still green but a light coating of frost shimmered on my car's windshield. There was frost on the gatepost and on the barbed wire. The road, the weeds in the ditch, the fence posts all the way to the highway gleamed silver in the sunlight.

Tom said, "Let's take the best way—not through Rawlins to the railroad but over Togwotee Pass and out past Jackson."

The Rawlins route is an unfriendly one that follows the Union Pacific and Interstate 80 through southwestern Wyoming and through the Red Desert. Tom's way was much more scenic. Our drive would take us northwest toward the mountains past the little mountain town of Dubois and into Jackson Hole.

The rugged scenery and combination of colors on that route is hard to describe: mountain maple, a bright crimson, against a backdrop of golden aspen and green Douglas fir, three colors together, crimson, bright yellow, and dark green. I glanced at Tom to say something about their beauty when I realized that the trees matched the colors in Tom's new bolo tie. The medallion had an outer ring of bright yellow beads, next to a smaller circle of deep red and a center of bright green.

"Nice tie," I said.

"Sure is. My daughter Marian made it. Say, did I ever tell you long time ago I had another friend named Johnson?"

I shook my head. "No."

"Johnson and I used to hold peyote meetings together up in Idaho when I lived there years ago. That's why I call you Johnson. You're like Johnson was to me, years ago."

"Will I meet him?" I asked.

"He's been gone for many years," he said.

My red Plymouth was crawling slower and slower on all six cylinders and my foot on the accelerator reached the floor. We'd passed the town of Dubois and were now going over Togwotee Pass which is the Continental Divide, elevation over nine thousand feet, and my hands instinctively gripped the steering wheel a little tighter. Togwotee, Tom said, was a big chief of the Mountain Shoshone, the *doyahin*. He lived in the Jackson Hole country until his band was moved down to a remote area of the reservation years ago. Members of his family still lived on the reservation and kept the old ways.

The spectacular Teton Range loomed on our right and herds of antelope and an occasional moose grazed on our left as we descended into Jackson Hole country. At a café in Jackson, we stopped for a hamburger and fries and, on the way out of town, the road followed the winding Snake River through its deep gorge as it coursed out into Idaho on its long route to the Pacific. Mountains gave way to the farm fields of eastern Idaho, wheat stubble and bright green alfalfa in all directions. Within another hour or so, the sun had begun to set and we were in Fort Hall.

Fort Hall had been a fur-trading post in the old days. It didn't have the impressive stone quarters for soldiers and barns for cavalry horses of Fort Washakie. All Fort Hall Agency had were agency buildings, a clinic, an old mission church and cemetery, and a cluster of government employees' frame houses. The Indians' houses were scattered beyond.

We drove down one gravel road, then up another, and as I was about to ask if we were lost, Tom suddenly said, "Stop." He motioned to a woman at the door of a small, unpainted frame house on the right side of the road. She was wiping her hands on her faded blue apron.

"That's my niece, Laura," Tom said.

Laura was short and sturdy and had a kind, smiling face round like the full moon. She was white-haired and her weathered complexion had been

4. An older log house at Fort Hall, Idaho, 1969.

burnished by the sun. She wore a flowered house dress under her apron and walked toward us with a shuffle.

"I'm sure glad to see both of you," she said. "I just made some good fry bread for supper. Come on in and have some after that long drive from Wyoming."

We followed her into her front room. There was no wallpaper, just wallboard and hung on the walls were family photos, none the same as in Tom's house. All at once, I became conscious of the smell of coffee. Tom scuffed his boots on a mat by the door and I moved to the side and looked around. A young woman sat on the blue plaid sofa. She was very pregnant. I nodded to her; she nodded back. A couple of easy chairs were nearby and, in the corner, a brown Coleman gas stove. Under a window with cheerful white curtains was a dining room table and chairs. A platter of fry bread was on the table.

Laura sprinkled sugar on two pieces of fry bread and handed them to us. They were still warm. Tom put his nose to his piece of fry bread and smelled. He took a big, hungry bite. I took one, too. The fry bread was soft and warm and sweet like a doughnut. Laura brought us coffee from the kitchen and we sat in the living room, Laura and Tom in the two easy chairs and me and the niece on the couch. Tom and Laura were talking back and forth, as people do when they're catching up.

"How's Cindy?" Tom asked, shifting into English and looking over at us. "We mean to put up good meeting for you, Cindy. I wanted to come over from Wyoming to help you all."

"The baby's coming any day now, Gramps," Cindy said.

A young man with a military crew cut came in from outside. My eye fell on his military crew cut. That had to be Benny, Tom's relative who was going to Vietnam. The Shoshone have a strong tradition of military service, beginning in World War I. Defending the United States was the same as defending the Shoshone, as one of my friends back in Wyoming put it. I decided not to mention I had filed as a conscientious objector to war before coming out West. The Cold War of conflicting ideology and power led to a hot war every once in a while between the superpowers. The result was the same, just grinding up people and soldiers. None of the members of Congress risked their lives over it. Neither did their sons. My draft board decided not to grant me the objector status. I wasn't a longtime member of one of the historic peace churches like the Quakers.

The nephew got himself a mug of coffee from the kitchen, then a piece of fry bread before he sat down in Laura's empty chair. Between swallows, he explained that he'd been working today for a local farmer in the potato harvest.

Laura was setting out a good meal on the table. We sat down to beans, more fry bread, mashed potatoes and gravy, and coffee. There was sweet potato pie and vanilla ice cream for dessert, a treat made just for us, Laura said.

"Cindy's due any day now and I've got orders to report for duty at the end of this coming week," Benny said. "I sure am glad you came to see us, Gramps. How about a couple of hands of penny-ante poker?"

Tom's smile flashed white against his dark skin. "I could use a little extra cash," he laughed.

A stack of coins later, Tom said to Benny, "We'll have good meeting. Can you be fireman while Cindy gets water in the morning?"

"Sure. I've done it before," Benny said, straightening a little in his chair. It was an honor to be fireman, to keep the fire burning all night in the teepee. "We invited some friends, people you already know from way back and some new friends of mine who believe on this medicine, this peyote," he said.

Laura motioned to the couch as a place for Tom to sleep. She put down a couple of folded blankets for him and I unrolled my sleeping bag on the floor. The Coleman stove that heated the small room burned low and the smell of supper lingered in the air. I took off my boots and got into the sleeping bag without undressing. My backpack was my pillow. In the kitchen, Laura was moving around.

I woke to the smell of fresh coffee and the sound of Benny's voice saying softly, "Wake up, dude. Gramps needs to sleep some more but you come right on into the kitchen."

It was warm and snug in the sleeping bag but overnight the floor had grown progressively harder and that coffee was smelling good. I climbed out and pulled on my boots.

"You're a Johnson, too?" Benny said. We were standing in the small kitchen. I nodded, staring blankly at the kitchen window, still not awake. On the window ledge were some clay flower pots with peyote cactus growing in them.

"We have a whole clan of Johnsons here," Benny said, pouring me a mug of coffee.

"People call us *Two Toms* back in Wyoming," I said, "but your grandpa told me he calls me Johnson after his friend from up here."

"Two Toms," he repeated. "It's a name for both of you. I like that. I came over to Wind River just for Grandpa Tom's Sun Dance a couple years ago 'cause I knew I was headed for Vietnam sooner or later. I knew I'd need those prayers."

I took a sip of the coffee. It was strong and warm. After batching for over a month, I was enjoying not having to cook.

"A guy down in Wind River said he was in a German prisoner of war camp during World War II," I said. "He says peyote songs and Sun Dance prayers saved his life. He used to sing them in his mind, you know," I said.

"Singing is a prayer to *Dam Apë* and you get power from it," Benny agreed.

"I'll be in the meeting with you," I said. "I'll be praying that you will come back safe and see all your family soon." With the back of his hand, Benny wiped at his eyes, then coughed uneasily. I heard Laura's shuffle on the linoleum.

"Is that *sugupuh*, that old man, awake yet? We need to talk," she said.

Tom made stirring noises in the other room and soon he was dressed for breakfast, straightening his new bolo tie as he came into the kitchen. As a doctor, he always wore dress pants and a freshly-pressed shirt.

Benny helped Tom to coffee and we moved to the dining table. Laura was dishing up breakfast.

"I've got short ribs ready to boil for supper," she told us, bringing out plates of eggs and hash browns. "We can always get some elk meat from the locker for lunch tomorrow. If you want coffee, it's in the kitchen."

I followed her into the kitchen with my mug. A kettle steamed on the stove. Laura took out a jar and put a handful of what looked like ground sage into a large aluminum teapot. I knew it had to be ground peyote. Peyote tea is milder and easier to digest than ground-up peyote buttons but the brown liquid is still bitter. At the peyote meeting, a small amount of it would be drunk after eating the dried and ground-up peyote.

The water had come to a furious boil. Laura filled the teapot and an acrid smell began to fill the room. She called to Tom, "I've got plenty of canned fruit, beef jerky, and creamed corn for the morning breakfast."

"*Deevee zhant.* You got everything we need," he called back.

After breakfast, Benny motioned to me to follow him out back. The teepee where the meeting was to be held was already up. It was plain it had been used for meetings many times because of the soot that layered the flaps at the top. Those flaps are called *nengk* or "ears." Inside, the floor was smooth and hard-pan clay with a few tufts of grass.

"I'm going to build the moon now," Benny said, his breath forming a cloud in the chill morning air. To a mound of red clay, he added some water and kneaded the mixture, smoothing it into a crescent-shaped mound. A clay mounded crescent always stands as an altar at the back of the peyote teepee.

Bringing in firewood was the next task. That was only a matter of carrying in a couple of piles of sticks because kindling had already been specially prepared for the meeting. Of the several kinds of peyote meetings, this was to be a cross-fires meeting. The flame would burn where the sticks crossed and more sticks would be added always in the same pattern. The cross-fires flame would produce the only light in the teepee during the long, all-night meeting.

"We'll bring this wood into the teepee and leave another pile just outside. We won't ever run out," Benny said. He paused, then said abruptly, "I want to tell you, I don't believe in this war. It's too far away and America is not in danger."

Benny told me how he had already gone through basic training and how his army butch haircut wasn't consistent with the war protestors' long hair but then, he had no choice: he was already in the army and the protestors were not. Some of them were younger Shoshone guys. They were growing their hair long, like the college students.

"We'll be there forever," I said.

Benny shrugged. "I just hope I come home in one piece."

Everyone knew more than one someone who had been killed over there. Three of my high-school friends had already been killed. I decided to change the subject. "Anything else I can do to prepare for the meeting?" I asked.

"Just follow everything Gramps tells you and pray with everyone tonight and you'll be all right," Benny said, rubbing his hands together to warm up. "Let's go inside the house."

Lunch came and went and it began to rain. It was a good idea to take a nap, Tom told me: the evening ahead would be a long one. Everyone would be up until sunrise. I lay down on my sleeping bag on the living room floor and listened to the patter of raindrops on the tin roof and Tom's snores.

I woke with a start. The rain had stopped. Tom was up again. He had gotten out his peyote box, his staff, and sash and fan. He was opening a bag of dried peyote buttons and Laura was watching him.

"I'll grind the peyote in my old coffee grinder," she said.

Tom handed her his bag of peyote buttons. He went on taking out things, his staff and fan of woodpecker feathers, and laying them on the arm of the couch.

The front door opened, the sound suddenly breaking into the quiet of the late afternoon. A middle-aged man walked in. He looked like a logger just getting off work, with his Red Wing boots, plaid shirt, and tan corduroys.

"Hey, Alfred!" Tom called to him.

"Time for a good prayer meeting tonight," the man said, rubbing his hands together. "I'm ready for a good meeting. I heard you was leading, Tom, so I wanted to join you."

Tom had stopped laying out his things. "I'm peyote chief tonight and you will be good assistant, just like all the times before with you and me."

"I've got some new peyote songs I learned when I stayed with the Comanches in Oklahoma," Alfred said.

With the arrival of Tom's assistant, everything seemed to be ready for the meeting. We had a light supper of bread and meat and after, Tom held up his hands, saying a prayer, asking that everyone in the house be blessed and that the meeting be a good one, for a good purpose.

People were starting to arrive now. I walked over to the window overlooking the backyard. Benny had started a fire in the teepee. It burned brightly, a yellow flame between two crossed sticks just beyond the teepee's entrance. The inside of the teepee glowed.

Soon, the teepee was filled with friends and relatives. We sat cross-legged on blankets on the ground inside, talking in low voices, waiting. Some had brought straight canes maybe three feet long with brilliant beaded decorations and gourd rattles, also beaded. Alfred went to the back of the teepee and Tom joined him. Both of them had put on dark suit jackets, and over those they wore scarlet sashes.

"We are all gathered here," Tom began in Shoshone, "for a good prayer meeting to ask *Dam Apë* to bless Cindy and her baby and keep them from harm." No one except Tom spoke now. "We also want to ask *Dam Apë* to bless Benny and keep him safe while he's in Vietnam."

"*Dam Apë*," Alfred said, "have mercy on us poor Indians who are humble in seeking God's help and guidance over the rough places in life."

A fresh peyote button is a small green cactus about the size of a quarter. Tom placed one on the middle of the earthen crescent Benny had made that morning. The meeting had begun.

A man began to beat rapidly on a little cast-iron drum no larger than a small saucepan. The drum had water in it, I knew. In the water were pieces of charcoal. To keep the sound deep and resonant, the drummer must keep wetting the top of the drum. This is done by tilting the drum. The water splashes inside the drum and wets the drumhead from underneath.

Alfred knelt. He held a staff in his right hand and a gourd rattle in his left. He began to shake the rattle in time with the beat of the drum. His song was a long, high-pitched melody. Syllables, not words, tumbled from Alfred's lips in the place of words. He finished his song and the drummer passed the drum to the next person. Again, the beat began. A second singer got to his knees. He held his staff in his right hand and shook his gourd rattle to the beat with his other hand, like Alfred had. The drum made its way around the teepee, passing the women by. They sat in silence with their heads bowed as each man took his turn kneeling, singing, shaking his rattle. The drum even came my way but I did not know any peyote songs, nor did I have a staff or gourd rattle, so I passed.

Now the drum had come back to Tom. He put it aside. "*Dam Apë*, we ask your blessings on this meeting again, that we can all come together and join for a good purpose. That purpose is to ask you to shower your blessings on Cindy and Benny," he prayed. He picked up a small bowl and spooned out a dark green powder into the palm of his hand. It was ground peyote. He spat onto it and mixed the saliva into the powder to form a large marble of peyote. This he ate.

The bowl of powder made its way around the circle. This time, the women took part. Paper cups of peyote tea followed. No one said much, only a murmured "Here," as the bowl was passed or a low "Thank you." The Shoshone believe that peyote is a gift from the Creator. It is a sign of the Creator's power when ingested. Peyote is bitter like bitter herbs, like ground-up parsley and sage. The bitter peyote is a sign of suffering, Tom had told me, and the entire group was suffering for Benny and Cindy. Peyote was given by God to help the Indian people bear their suffering. It was, as Tom explained to me later, like a messenger signifying *Dam Apë*'s presence in the peyote meeting. Always, people refer to peyote not as "it" but as "he" or "him," as if peyote were a living being sent by God.

The songs were becoming richer and more penetrating, colors more vivid, the scent of the wood fire more pungent. Wave after wave of joy washed over me. Was it my imagination or were the men singing better and louder?

Cindy and Benny were kneeling next to Tom. With his eagle feather fan, he brushed them on the head, the shoulders, the arms, the legs. Tom's voice came across as more of a song than a speech.

"*Dam Apë*," he said/sang, "bless and keep Benny in all of his travels as he goes to war. Protect Cindy and her baby."

All the lives being destroyed by this war! Tears clouded my gaze. I glanced at the woman next to me. Tears had found their way down her cheeks. Around the teepee, men and women were tearing up. The lead singer's voice grew louder and more insistent.

More peyote and peyote tea followed and, several hours later after prayers, more peyote made its way around again. There were four rounds of peyote, all told. Four is the sacred number of the four directions of the universe—north, east, south, west—and between the singing and the prayers and the peyote, it seemed a short while until the gray light of dawn was filtering through the teepee's canvas.

Tom stood. "I prayed. I asked *Dam Apë* and our elder brother Jesus for mercy. Be with Benny and Cindy, I asked, as they face their trials in the future, tomorrow or soon to come," he said.

Heads nodded. "Uhm," came the sound from around the teepee. It was the way Shoshones show their approval.

Cindy was waiting at the entrance to the teepee. She carried a tray with bowls and paper cups and knelt before the clay crescent moon of the altar. In the bowls were four sacred foods: fruit, corn, meat, and water. We each took a small amount of fruit, corn, and meat in a paper cup and a second cup with water, passing the foods around the circle, eating our ceremonial portion.

Tom raised his hands. "Thank you all for coming to the meeting," he said and his voice was hoarse from use. "Thank you for helping to put it up. Thank you, Alfred for helping me out. Thank you, Benny, for keeping the fire going all night. Thank you, Cindy, for being the water woman."

Cindy bowed toward Tom. She backed out, not turning from us until she reached the entrance to the teepee.

Tom took the peyote button off the center of the moon altar. The meeting was over.

Now it was okay to talk, to laugh, to visit. We had been sitting on the ground all night and now we stretched our legs, stood, started moving around. Some left the teepee, some stayed. One man said to no one in particular, "We Indians used to shoot the bull on horseback with bow and arrow. Now we're only bullshitters."

Snorts and low laughter.

Another said, "Once there was an old-time peyote chief. He was so serious he could never smile once, not even after meeting was over. People said his mouth was always in a frown. People said that frown was stitched on his face."

More laughter.

We were all laughing. The skin around Tom's eyes crinkled most at that last one about the frowning peyote chief.

"That was old White Horse, the father of *Bonhaits*, Skunk," Tom said. Everyone was looking his way. "He was a real *doyahin*, Mountain Sho-shone—tough people from up near Yellowstone Park. Good at catching lots of mountain sheep for dinner."

There was a pause in the conversation. Then one of the younger men blurted out, "I'm sick and tired of this war in Vietnam!"

Heads bobbed up and down in agreement.

"When the Japanese attacked us, we had to fight," said a middle-aged man. "I never saw any reason to fight the Viet Cong."

"There are going to be a lot of war widows after this one and I'm already one," a young woman said.

One of the lead singers said, "I'm tired of it, too. I was in France and Germany and did my duty but I wouldn't want to enlist in this one. A lot of young men are coming home in those green body bags. And for what?"

"Benny just shouldn't have to go," an older woman said.

After that, no one said anything much. There was nothing more to say. The war was a big mistake and Benny just shouldn't have to go. I shouldn't have to go. No one should have to go. Tom hadn't said anything about the war, good or bad. I noticed he never voiced his own opinions when he was doctoring. He was supportive and kind. That was part of his professional-ism. That was an important part of the healing he had to offer.

More food came into the tipi. It was breakfast with lots of hot coffee and pounded jerked elk meat and fry bread with strawberry jam. The good food made everybody feel happier. We hadn't slept, not a one of us. It was the peyote keeping us awake, keeping us in the mood to visit and joke around all morning.

"Dinner!" Laura announced incredibly soon.

We got up, shook hands all around, and filed into the house. A large meal of boiled short ribs, fry bread, chokecherry gravy, potato salad, canned fruit, blackberry pie, and vanilla ice cream lay on the table for the taking. It was delicious.

Then people began to leave. Only Cindy, Benny, Laura, Tom, and I were left. That afternoon and into the night we all slept that wonderful, peaceful sleep that only comes after having created a ceremony to bring everyone together to ask for help. It was the group and its support that helped everybody who knew Benny and Cindy, allowing them to vent their frustrations at the stupidity of the war.

The next morning, Benny and I were up early, chopping wood for a fire. The day was warm for October and the sun shone brightly, and Tom wanted us to have a sweat in the small sweat lodge behind the teepee. The lava rocks in the pit in the middle of the lodge were soon red-hot. Benny splashed water on them to make steam. The steam fell on my back and shoulders and I sat bolt upright. That steam was hot.

"Wowser!" said Tom. "That was a hot one."

Benny splashed water once, twice, four times, each hotter than the last.

"We pray now," Tom said. "We pray now to *Dam Apë* for all of us here. We are humble and we beg you to have mercy on us. Bless Benny here especially as he goes to war. Bless all of us who need help in every way. Bless the mountains, rocks, hills, rivers, and all living things."

Again, Benny splashed the water on the hot rocks four times.

"We all feel good, *zah nisunga*," Tom said. "Had good meeting, good sweat. Help each other. That's the Indian Way. Help each other."

4

ANOTHER WAY

TOM AND I HADN'T BEEN BACK FROM IDAHO FOR LONG WHEN THE WEATHER took a turn for the worse. More days than not, the clouds hung black and low. Some days, sleet coated the road in an icy glaze. It was easier to do our grocery shopping at the general store on the reservation than to drive into Lander. The general store at Wind River was around the bend and down the highway from Tom's place. It's still there. The store is well-stocked with clothing, hats, belts, magazines, large bags of flour and sugar, packages of lard and bacon, bulk sizes of cans and jars of just about every common food like fruit, beans, and vegetables, and large bottles of ketchup.

The particular morning I have in mind, when we walked in, Vinnie, the cashier, was wiping down her conveyor belt with a paper towel. A testy woman named Angela, who I knew was some relation to Doreen, was stocking a display of flannel shirts. Walt, the butcher, and a man I didn't know were standing by the door opposite the checkout. Walt was nodding and the man was talking low to him, his arms folded over his chest. I noticed them because Walt was fat and the man with him thin with a deeply lined face.

As we walked past, the man said, "How you doin', Tom? Who's this young *duiwichee taivo* here?"

Tom stopped. "This here's Tom, too, who stays with me and is learning from me."

The man looked me over. "I'm Louie, Tom's cousin. You've got a good teacher," he said.

I made some noises about how, yes, I was very lucky to have such a good teacher.

"You putting up any more Sun Dances?" Louie asked Tom.

"I'm retired from leading Sun Dances," Tom said, "but I still put up peyote meetings and we still have sweats over at my place. You ought to come over sometime."

Louie sighed. "I've tried just about every religion," he said. "Our grandparents were Catholics and I was strong in peyote for a long time with my wife's people. But now I've found the church I think I really belong in. You should come over to one of our meetings. We have them at my house and most of my family, they come."

"I'd sure like to do that," Tom said. "I'd sure like to visit your church. There's all kinds of churches and I go and pray with everybody."

Louie looked pleased. "We've got another meeting tomorrow. There's going to be a new preacher from Colorado visiting us. Meeting starts at about three in the afternoon. Then we have dinner for everyone there."

Tom quirked an eyebrow at me. I nodded. It would be interesting to go. "We'll be there," Tom said.

On the way home, he told me that Louie's dad was his uncle. The man had died in a terrible accident when he was still young. Louie and his brothers and sisters were raised by relatives, including Tom's mother's brother. Tom and Louie's grandparents, John and Julia Enos, had migrated from Montana about 1870 at the invitation of Washakie when the reservation opened. They were Flathead and Iroquois, not Shoshone, Tom told me. Chief Washakie was himself Flathead on his mother's side, and his mother was a sister to John Enos's mother.

This was the only time I ever heard Tom talk about a relative who had died. He never talked about his deceased wife, Helen. His son Tommy once told me that his dead mother had appeared to him in a dream and had beckoned him to come with her. That dream was so powerful that Tommy needed a sweat ceremony to ask for special blessings. In traditional Shoshone culture, once someone was dead and buried, that person was never spoken of again. People believed that the spirit of that person might return and have some kind of power over you, even to the point of influencing you to join them in the afterlife.

"Louie's a good man," Tom said. "His wife's family are good peyote people. I knew them well. We go to his prayer meeting and have good time. Let's ghost."

We stopped at the Sacajawea Service Station to fill up. The same people who owned the general store owned the service station. It was an A-frame building, a newly popular style, and its namesake was the heroine of the Lewis and Clark Expedition. Some said she came back to live out her last years with the Wind River Shoshone.

"I'm putting up a sweat this afternoon," Tom said as I pulled in. In those days, there was no self-service. A uniformed attendant filled your tank and washed your windows. All Tom and I had to do was sit in the car and pay for it afterward. Today Sam Timbe was working. His dad lived up Trout Creek Road from Tom's place.

"Fill her up and check the oil," I told Sam.

Tom chuckled and I looked at him, surprised. He was grinning.

"What?" I asked.

"Fill her up, Wants-A-Woman," Tom laughed.

I had been hoping Tom was in the process of dropping that little nickname. He hadn't used it in the past couple of weeks. "I'll do everything I can to help out with the sweat," I said to change the subject.

We watched Sam lift the windshield wipers away from the windshield. He squirted window cleaner on the glass.

"My son Tommy can chop wood for the fire and carry hot lava rocks," Tom said. "That's the hard part. All you have to do is light the fire."

It turned out that Tommy was busy that day checking out an irrigation gate in Tom's back forty. I was the only one around to prepare the sweat lodge for Tom's friends. The sweat lodge was on the other side of Tom's house. A big pile of pine and cottonwood logs sat next to it. Periodically, someone would show up at Tom's with a load of sawed logs. I needed to take an axe to them, one by one, splitting each in half lengthwise. It was hard work and, partway through, I took off my heavy flannel shirt and hung it on the branch of a nearby willow. The sky had cleared. The sun shone bright.

I had built other sweats for Tom. I knew to pile the wood around a nest of volcanic rocks, to douse a little kerosene on the wood so it would burn quick and hot. It takes about half an hour for the wood to burn down until nothing is left but embers and red hot rocks.

Tom's friends had begun arriving. I had been in many sweats but today I was the fireman. This particular day, I preferred being fireman to being a participant. Someone had to keep the rocks heated and I was younger by decades than anyone else around the house today. This might be the last time I could do this for Tom before winter snows and subzero weather would arrive. It was my job to stand outside and make sure there were enough hot rocks to heat the lodge, my job to take the spent rocks out and replace them with more hot ones.

5. Tom Wesaw's sweat lodge near his house on Trout Creek, 1969.

The lodge, a dome-shaped tent, sat about fifty feet behind Tom's house and a few paces from the fire. It was a frame of willow branches with a covering of old canvas and rugs to keep the heat inside. The tent flap was an old rug, too. Tom had lifted it and flung it over the top of the lodge; it was heavy enough to stay in place. He and his friends were already taking off their heavy overalls and flannel shirts and hanging them on the willow's branches. When they had stripped down to their shorts, they went into the lodge to sit down on rugs placed over the hard-packed dirt floor.

"We need some hot rocks, Johnson," Tom called.

I hoisted a shovelful of red-hot rocks and walked it carefully to the lodge. In the middle of the lodge was a shallow pit. I tipped the shovel and the hot rocks slid into it. It took two shovelfuls to fill the hole. Every fifteen minutes or so, I was to come back to the lodge to remove cool rock and replace it with hot. It wasn't especially hard work and now that the fire had burned down, I put my flannel shirt back on. Every now and then, I shoveled some of the ashes over the rocks outside to keep them warm, but

6. Tommy Wesaw, Tom's son, lighting the fire to heat rocks for the sweat lodge, 1969.

mostly I leaned on my shovel and listened to the songs from inside the lodge.

Tom always began the ceremony by dipping a bundle of willow branches in a pail of hot water and splashing them on the hot rocks. This produced a heavy steam. Then he and each of the other men prayed.

After the ceremonial number of four songs and four different splashings, along with prayers from each of the men in the lodge, Tom opened the flap covering the door of the lodge. The men filed out. They stood outside in their gym shorts, rubbing the sweat on their arms and their chests while I hurried to replenish the cooler rocks with hot ones from the pile outside. This done, Tom motioned for them to go back in. After the fourth repetition of the ceremony, the men came out and put on their clothes and the sweat was over.

Tom closed the flap over the door after them, stood, and, his elbows cocked to the side, put his palms flat on his chest. "Wowser," he said. "That was sure a good one. You made those rocks really hot, Johnson."

Tom's sweat was made with the hottest rocks. I appreciated the compliment. It made me feel good, like I had made a real contribution. Tom's sweats never held more than six or eight. They were always filled with prayers and songs and were part of Tom's ministry to his people. They were completely different from the kind of New Age sweats held by those who charge money for them. In 2009, for example, fifty people paid between nine and fifteen thousand dollars each to participate in a sweat in Sedona, Arizona. At last count, three died from excessive heat. Tom would have been appalled to hear of this crass commercialization of a deeply spiritual ceremony.

The next day arrived, rainy and cold. Tom had the weather report on the local radio station. The local radio weatherman, Ivan McGee, said it would be cloudy all day with snow flurries.

Tom grunted. "McGee is usually wrong. I can predict the weather better than those weathermen. Their predictions are full of baloney. It's November and, sure enough, the weather will be cold but there will be no snow. I think that McGee is wrong about the sun. The sun will come out this afternoon just about the time we go to Louie's for the meeting. That will be a good sign that his meeting will help everyone who came."

The pink phone rang and I went to turn down the radio.

"Hi, Loreena!" Tom was saying. "I sure wish I could be there but I can't get a ride to Montana. If I could, I'd be there as soon as I can. I'm going to pray for you today, though. I'll buy some beads and send them on to you."

When Tom got off the phone, I said, "I'll drive you to Montana, if you want."

"It's a long trip up to Havre in northern Montana this time of year. Hundreds of miles. I wouldn't ask you to drive me that far. The roads are bad with all the snow in the mountains. My granddaughter is having a baby and wants me to put up a meeting. I can't even ask her husband to meet me half way at Crow Agency. It's not right for him to leave his family right now," Tom said.

After lunch, Tom put on his best trousers, a bright blue dress shirt, and his favorite bolo tie. He dashed cologne on his face and announced he was ready to leave for Louie's place. It was already almost three. In the car, Tom held a pumpkin pie on his lap. Tom had bought it the day before to take to the meeting.

We drove past the Fort Washakie School. That prompted Tom's memory about his granddaughter who had called from Montana. Tom had picked her up many times after school when she was a little girl so she wouldn't have to ride the school bus so long.

"You and Louie are part Flathead, right?" I asked.

"From our grandparents," Tom said.

"And Louie's part Flathead and his wife is Arapaho. So what tribe do Louie's kids belong to?" I asked.

"They're enrolled Shoshone," Tom said. "There are good reasons why Louie would want his children enrolled as Shoshone, not Arapaho. The Shoshones are a much smaller tribe than the Arapaho so our money from the oil under the ground is larger. The money from the reservation was divided in half between the two tribes after all the claims against the government were settled, you know. Also, the Arapahos have a rule for enrolling children. If the father wasn't Arapaho, the kids can't be enrolled. Louie's wife is Arapaho but he's a Shoshone so their kids can only be enrolled as Shoshone. The Shoshone have known for a very long time that mixed marriages between tribes were common in our history, and so we say that a child can be enrolled Shoshone if only one parent was already enrolled as Shoshone. Part of Indian ancestry of the other tribe would be added into the kid's Shoshone ancestry and the kid's mixed Indian ancestry would now simply be called "Shoshone." We Shoshones want to make sure all kids of mixed tribal background would not lose their Indian ancestry when they're enrolled. We're all mixed up but we still call ourselves Shoshone."

What Tom said made sense. All of sudden, I realized it was sunny. "The weather," I said.

"Yeah, it's sunny," he shrugged. "Just as I said it would be. The old Indians like my uncle taught me how to predict the weather better than ol' Ivan McGee on the radio any day."

I glanced at him skeptically.

"I feel the change of weather in my bones, Johnson, and the moon is like a cradle on its side holding water. That means dry weather," he said.

Louie's small ranch was strung along the side of a blacktopped road. Two barking dogs milled alongside the car while I parked. Singing drifted from the house. The dogs escorted us and the pumpkin pie to the back-door but they didn't follow us into the kitchen.

Everyone was in the front room singing a gospel hymn. Tom put his pie down on the counter and we waited in the kitchen until the song was over.

In the living room, a row of folding chairs held about twelve people. We slid into two empty chairs. The preacher read the passage from the

Book of Acts about the first Pentecost when the Holy Spirit appeared in tongues of fire to Jesus's disciples after the resurrection. The people, filled with the Holy Spirit at the sight, spoke in tongues, the preacher read.

"I'm here from Colorado to organize a church of believers in the Pentecostal speaking in tongues," the preacher said. "I was raised to believe you need a church you can respond to, a church that lets you, encourages you, wants to help you experience the Holy Spirit and what it can do to change your life. There are so many of us here, everywhere, whose lives need to be changed from being unperfected to perfected. That means turning your life around, becoming a better person, lifting yourself up, joining this church!"

Everyone seemed interested. I looked over at Tom. He looked back at me, pressed his lips together, and nodded.

"You will be able to speak in tongues, just like in the days of the disciples," the preacher said. "It will change your life. You will know what it's like to be holy before God, to have all your sins forgiven and come to Jesus the spotless Lamb of God."

"Blblblbuhblblbl-buh-blblblbl," an older woman called out. It was not an English word and it didn't sound like Shoshone, either.

"Doodahdooodeeeoooo-weeeah doodahdooodeeeoooo-weeeah," a younger woman next to her started in.

"Nooonahneeooeeooonah," Louie said over and over.

The room was filled with sound. Almost everyone was speaking in tongues, except Tom and me. Tom sat still and respectfully silent. As for myself, I didn't feel overcome with the Holy Spirit.

"I know that I'm saved!" a woman cried out in English. "Praise the Lord!"

"The Spirit is with us, in this house, in this very room!" a man exclaimed.

The talking in tongues died down in fits and starts. First one person would stop, then another, but that first one might start up again.

When the room had mostly quieted, Louie stood. "I'd like all of you to give what you can to help pay the traveling costs of this young man who came all the way from Denver, Colorado, to help us organize a church," Louie said. "Anything you can do will help and be much appreciated. Our goal is to build a log church on some deeded land I have near the Fort. The church will be round and shaped like a big Sun Dance lodge and healing will take place in it. The Holy Spirit and Jesus Christ will appear in that church and bless and heal many. Receive the Holy Spirit and your life will be changed forever."

Tom leaned over to me and whispered, "That church is all right. It does the same thing as our peyote church and our Sun Dance and wants to bless and heal people, too. It's just another way and I like it."

Tom the Listener

Most gambling at Wind River involved card games like poker or monte and took place at individual homes or at the corrugated metal building near the Fort known as Little Lost Vegas. In his younger years Tom had been an expert card player, but without a car, getting to Little Lost Vegas wasn't easy. He never asked me to take him there. Instead, the gambling came to him.

One day, after a couple of early December snowstorms, the temperature fell to zero. That afternoon after the plow had come through and cleared the road, Joe Lafferty, who lived a mile or so up Trout Creek, stopped by to visit. Tom called him Joe Laugh-at-Me. Like Tom, Joe was a recent widower. Also like Tom, he didn't mind a game or two of poker.

Joe wasn't a very tall man but he had muscular arms and shoulders under his faded work shirt. He always wore a bolo tie with a large, rough-cut turquoise in it. Joe visited often as the weather turned colder. His visits followed a pattern: first, chewing tobacco and talk, next dinner and more talk, then poker. We never went to his house; Joe never had invited us. Besides, Tom and I were taking good care of ourselves as bachelors. Tom's family kept us well supplied with meat and fresh trout and baked cakes and pies. Friends and clients often repaid Tom with food. I had learned to make fry bread. We didn't have to resort to spam sandwiches or canned tuna. My mashed potatoes and pork-chop gravy, canned peas, beans, and corn were plenty good.

"I never was much of a cook," Joe told us between sips of coffee. "I live on fried egg and spam sandwiches, baked beans and bacon and drink a lot of coffee."

"Why don't you eat with us tonight and we'll play some cards after supper," Tom said. It was what he always said to Joe. Joe was lonely and needed someone to talk to. Tom was very good at listening. Listening was a large part of what he did as a doctor.

"I'll take you up on that invitation, if you don't mind," Joe said. It was what he always said to Tom. Then, like always, he pulled out a dark blue tin of Key chewing tobacco from his hip pocket, opened it, and laid it on the table.

"I like a chaw of tobacky sometimes," he said, taking a pinch of it between his thumb and forefinger. "Helps to settle the old stomach." Joe put the pinch in his mouth. With his tongue, he moved the wad of tobacco to his right cheek.

It was already four o'clock and starting to get dark. I got up and opened the refrigerator. In the meat keeper were some elk steaks that one of Tom's nieces had given us.

"I'll fry up some steaks and we'll put those together with mashed potatoes and gravy and corn and beans and have a pretty decent supper," I said.

I knew Joe was eyeing the food I was taking out. He said, "You two guys, Two Toms, you'll have to come up to my place some time. I'm still pretty good, even though I've got this arthritis in my knee. It nags at me. You know, Millie got kinda poorly, and she had cancer and was ailin' so the clinic sent her to Casper for an operation, but they got it too late and she never really recovered. She was only sixty-two—died just a year ago."

It was the first time Joe had invited us to his place. I knew Tom wouldn't go because Joe's wife had died there.

"I remember Millie real well," Tom said. "She was real pretty and she used to go to forty-nine dances we had down at the old tribal dance hall." He looked over at me. "Forty-nine dances are when you dance in a circle. They had some good dances in those days—not like now. There's nothing to do on the reservation anymore and the young folks just go into town."

"That's how I met her, at those forty-nine dances," Joe said. "When those forty-nine dances started to get popular, I was a young stud. I used to come down to the Fort on Saturday night after a hard week of ropin' those calves. I was workin' on the old Em-bar Ranch in the Owl Creeks. I'd come to Wyomin' hearin' there was work out here. I was out of South Dakota, and I'm enrolled back there. I'm a quarter Sioux but never was part of the tribe. Millie and I hit it off right away. We went to dances every week. Just like me, she was a breed but she was Shoshone and before long, we tied the knot. Went to the Justice of the Peace in Lander. That was durin' Prohibition when the only way you could get a drink was through your bootlegger. Remember them days, Tom?"

Tom nodded.

"I thought that we could really make a go of it," Joe said, "what with her allotment and some range land next to it that we got to rent from the tribe. I had a good couple of dozen steers at one time. We had a good living for some years. Had my own brand, too—the Lazy L. Then we got that Tunison Judgment money. Remember, Tom?"

Tom grunted. "Sure do," he said. "The government owed us for placing the Arapahos on our reservation back in the early days. We had a smart lawyer with that Mr. Tunison but still it took us years to get the government to pay the money they owed us. We did get about fifteen hundred dollars apiece but it was like pulling teeth. Uncle Sam took out money from the judgment for gifts and supplies they gave us. They even took out money for a saddle they gave Chief Washakie. So I took my fifteen hundred and I added a room to our house, a new stove, and got a used car that could really run."

"Well, with that judgment money, Millie and I bought some steers and a Ford pickup," Joe said. "We thought we'd be in the ranching business, and for the next few years, during the war, we did real well. Then prices fell and I got a bum leg. Couldn't rope or brand cattle so we sold them off. After that we had her per capita to live on and any other work I could get around the reservation, and that's about it. I'm sure glad the tribe and the government could help her through her last illness, the cancer. If it hadn't been for the tribe and the Indian Health Service, we wouldn't have had no help at all. Those Arapahos were darn lucky to be put here. Wind River has lots of oil and gas. It's given them a better living than they would ever have had if they'd been placed on the Pine Ridge reservation in South Dakota where I come from. No oil or gas out there."

Tom nodded. "The reservation's money was split right down the middle. There's more Arapahos now than Shoshones, and the Arapahos are getting ahead of us in numbers."

"Millie and me never had much to do with either tribe," Joe said. "We used to go and visit the Shoshone Sun Dance and some of the other dances when they had the old dance hall, but we never camped out in no teepee or nothing. Millie's only a quarter Shoshone and I'm not part of this tribe. We was both raised Catholic. She went to church once in a while—Christmas and Easter—but I never went."

Joe leaned back in his kitchen chair and moved his wad of tobacco around in his mouth. Turning toward me, he said, "You're a young *taivo* and haven't been in these parts very long, but you know, I think this tribe's lost its spunk. I don't think they do very many dances anymore. Leastwise I haven't seen them."

The pink phone rang. Tom went to answer it. Joe said again, "I think this tribe's lost its spunk."

Nothing I had seen at Wind River made me think Joe was right about this. The Shoshone seemed to be doing a good job of keeping their community alive. They'd hired a good lawyer to help them out. I wondered if Joe's comment was due to a lack of interest in tribal matters. Perhaps it was just the way he felt now, after his wife's death. His ties to the tribe had never been that close. Joe was just depressed, maybe, and had a need to gripe about something.

Tom came back to the kitchen and said, "I just got a call from Montana. Loreena had a baby boy. Her husband Henry tells me they will have new three-bedroom house by next fall. You know, peyote saved Henry from alcohol some years ago."

"That's good to hear," I said. "I'll bet Loreena's real happy the baby's okay."

Tom smiled. "Sure wish I could go and see her, but that'll have to wait till next spring."

"I remember Loreena," Joe added. "Real nice girl. Pretty, too. She used to stay with you, didn't she? I think I might go back to South Dakota for a while. I've got a couple of half-brothers back there, married to breed Sioux. They work for some of them big ranchers near White River and Philip. I know they won't take me in, but I can stay for the rest of the winter in one of them motels rented by the month."

I started the supper and Tom and Joe talked on. Mostly, it was about ranching. I was busy putting flour, salt, and pepper on the elk steaks and starting to boil water for the potatoes. I opened a can of sweet corn and emptied it into a saucepan. I got out a couple of pieces of fry bread I had made yesterday, dipped them in sugar, and gave one to Joe. He spat out his wad of tobacco into the kitchen trash. I poured some more coffee for Tom.

After supper, we started our card game, with Tom dealing out the cards. Tom was a really good poker player. I hadn't played cards much for the last few years, and poker was never my best game. Joe always complained he'd lost his touch because he hadn't played much in later years. Neither Joe nor I ever won many hands, and Tom always ribbed me for not really trying. "You smart man, Johnson," he'd say with a sly grin. "You should try a little harder. Maybe you'll get better. You can't get worse."

Joe took a fresh chew of tobacco. "When I was just out of school, a couple years past the eighth grade, I horsed around just like all the young half-breed studs," he said. He was looking over his hand of cards. "This was up in South Dakota just off the reservation. We was all buddies and thought we was something, you know, just because we could stay on a bucking bronco for a few minutes or do some fancy roping. Well, one of those things we had to do was prove our manhood, you know."

Tom laughed. "Yep."

Joe said, "There was this lady in town who had a couple of girls living with her, sort of helping out with the housekeeping and such. She had a ranch to manage after her husband died, and there was a couple of wranglers who worked for her, too. She wasn't running no business, but those two girls, they was kinda wild. They came from Deadwood, in the Hills, and they had to leave for some reason. Now they was down our way. Well, one of the boys got wind of them, and told us how they needed some cash. He said maybe we could help them, you know. I was all for it—needed to prove I was a real man. So one night we all went out on the town and ended up at the Silver Dollar Saloon. A couple of the gals was there, and we started teasin' them and buyin' drinks. They liked that, and they was sure pretty. Well, one thing led to another, and there was a hotel right next to the saloon. My buddy was a couple of years older, and said that he'd pay for a room for himself and another for me, if that was okay, and we'd invite the gals to come along. We'd all had a couple of drinks by that time, and I took the younger gal to my room, and before long, we started lovin' and kissin' and one thing led to another and by golly, everything happened, and I diddled her good. I sure lived to regret it, though, 'cause I caught a case of the clap, and it was weeks before that was gone. My buddy had the same thing happen, and we both resolved to check out the opposite sex before we went out on a limb again." Joe had a big grin on his face.

Tom said, "You sure like the girls, Joe. You know what I call Johnson here is *Waipe Suguaint*."

Joe liked that. "Oh, I know what that means," he laughed.

I pretended to study my hand of cards.

"I'm over eighty years old and you're never too old to have a girl-friend," Tom said. "Mine is named Doreen, and she is sure beautiful. Right, Johnson?"

"You sure know how to pick them," I said, nodding. I knew for certain that Tom hadn't seen Doreen in quite some time.

Joe coughed a couple of times, lay his hand face down on the table, took out a blue and white handkerchief from his pants pocket, stuffed that back into his pocket, thought a moment, then pulled out a crooked cigar from his shirt pocket, the kind that was soaked in rum, and stood up to light it.

"You could find a woman, too, Joe," Tom said. "You're a lot younger than I am."

Joe drew on his cigar. The end glowed. He let out a cloud of smoke. "Maybe. I hear there's some good women up in Dubois. Think I'll go up there and take a look, go to some of the taverns and maybe stay a night or two."

He sat down again, cigar in one hand and took up his hand of cards. He laid down two cards.

Tom kept all his. He must have had a good hand again. When the hand was called, Tom laid his down on the table—two queens, a jack, and two kings. I only had a queen and a couple of tens and eights. Joe fared even worse. Tom corralled all the chips and he collected a couple of dollars and some cents from Joe and me. It was a typical game for the three of us.

"I need to call it a night," Joe said. "Tom, you have all that Injun luck, and I'm just a fake, a dime-store Indian. I'll get back my old savvy and beat you guys some other night. Come up and see me sometime. I've got a bottle of Old Crow and we three can try our luck again."

"Come see us again," Tom called as Joe let himself out of the house. It was past ten o'clock, one of those clear, intensely starry December nights that can only happen at a high altitude in an area uncluttered with city light pollution.

"I don't want to go to Joe's place," said Tom.

I thought I understood completely. Millie had died in that house. "I'll drop by sometime when it's daylight and invite him over again," I said.

A couple of days later I made some sandwiches and a thermos of coffee for Joe and drove up to see him. His small frame house was in a state of disrepair. He must have been adding on to it over the years. Piles of lumber and sawdust lay around, and as I went up to the door, Joe called out for me to come in.

The inside of the house was like the outside. Wall studs didn't have any wallboard over them. Plywood was tacked up here and there and the only furniture was an old bedstead with bedsprings and a stained mattress, a cot, a table with a radio on it, a kitchen table, a couple of chairs, and an electric frying pan. There were empty food cartons and tin cans and dust and cobwebs and sawdust all over. I stared at the sink full of crusted dishes a few moments, and then I gave Joe the sandwiches and coffee. I invited him back to play cards with us, just like I told Tom I would. I told Joe how sorry I was that his wife had died, imagining to myself that her long illness must have been responsible for the neglect and mess I saw all around me.

Joe was standing in the middle of that bereaved and desolate room. He nodded his thanks. "I'll drop by some evening if I see a light in the kitchen," he said.

He never came back. A couple of weeks later, after Christmas, I read in the local paper that Joe Lafferty had been found dead in his house. The heat had gone off and he must have frozen to death.

At least, that's what the paper said. Tom said, "Joe had no one else after Millie died—no friends, no family that cared about him. Joe wasn't a part of the tribe. He never tried to be one of us. You did a good thing to take him some food, Johnson. That was all you could do."

6

A Visit with Bill Shakespeare

In the few months I had been around, Tom and I had driven out to Toby's place three or four times, but even with medication and many trips to the hospital Toby kept getting weaker and weaker. He had a weak heart, what Tom called a "heart filled with blood" and what Western medicine calls congestive heart failure. He was only fifty years old.

Toby's son Victor was about my age and often came to peyote meetings. After one meeting, he told me how proud he was of his family. Victor's great-grandfather had been one of Chief Washakie's close advisors. Washakie's inner circle was known as *degwani*—speakers—in the Shoshone language. The government always referred to them as "sub-chiefs." Victor told me how he hated that term. "You're an anthropology student," he said. "You know that a sub-chief is a white man's word. A *degwani* was a man known for his speaking ability and leadership. The *degwani* didn't have any less power than Washakie himself. It was the government that decided to have one chief and then call the other men 'sub-chiefs.' Whites have always believed Washakie had more power than the others. That's not the way we were. Everybody had a say and the *degwani* were kind of like our council is today."

Whenever Victor called Tom on behalf of his dad, I felt for him. His dad was not going to get better. On this particular day, Tom looked sad as he spoke with Victor on the phone. When he hung up, Tom said, "Toby is a good man. Used to be peyote fireman and helped me with many meetings. He needs me again. We go."

Tom gathered up his peyote box with its cedar and fans and we drove to Toby's place over on North Fork Road. All you could see from the road were several old corrals that stood empty. Toby's house was long and low and built of logs in the older style. The house was close to the Little Wind River and almost hidden by willows.

Victor was waiting for us outside. "Dad's real sick," he said to me in English, and in Shoshone he said the same thing to Tom but with a few more words that described how his Dad felt. "Weak," he told Tom. "I think he's dying."

Through the small windows, the grey December light filtered into the small front room. The log walls had been painted white to make the room lighter. Clay pots filled with peyote cactus crowded the window-sills. There were several beds in the room and Toby lay on the one against the wall. He was propped up with pillows and covered with a Pendleton blanket. "Hey, Tom," he managed. "Glad you came."

Tom placed his hand gently on Toby's chest. I sat quietly in a chair that Victor offered me. Victor already had a cup of peyote tea ready; he handed it now to Tom. Tom placed the edge of the cup to Toby's lips. Toby opened his mouth as best he could but brown liquid ran down the side of his mouth.

Tom handed the cup back to Victor. He began brushing Toby with his eagle feather fan, starting with his head and working down toward his chest and abdomen. Toby's eyes closed. Tom prayed in Shoshone, "*Dam Apë*, our Father, have mercy on your sick child; *som Bavi Jesus*, our elder brother Jesus, be with him in his struggle with pain."

Victor sat on the edge of his father's bed. He placed his hand on his father's shoulder.

Tom was putting a match to some cedar in a dish and soon its fragrance filled the room. From his medicine box, he took out a bundle of sweet sage that he had saved from summer. He pressed it to Toby's chest several times.

"Pray with me, Victor and Johnson," Tom said.

I closed my eyes. Tom addressed *Dam Apë* in Shoshone. He asked Our Father to be with all of us during this difficult time. We sat like this for several minutes. Victor was crying softly.

Tom nudged me. I opened my eyes. He was standing, motioning with his head toward the door.

On the way home, Tom said, "I don't think Toby'll make it through another night. His heart is too weak. I couldn't make him better but I could help him know that *Dam Apë* is with him."

In the morning, Victor called to tell us his father had died and the wake would be that next evening. When we arrived, friends and relatives

7. Sacajawea Cemetery looking east toward Fort Washakie, 1970.

already crowded the room where we had been so recently. High, keening wails came from the women. Toby's body was laid out in a casket. Tom shook hands with relatives and then we sat for a while, visiting in low voices. Victor asked Tom and several others to offer prayers.

Soon after, we left. Tom didn't say much on the way home but when I had parked the car under the big cottonwood in front of Tom's house, he said, "I've helped bury many of them, many Shoshone people. You know, Johnson, many people died from TB years ago. Today it's from heart failure or maybe from pneumonia or cancer. Some people live long time. But a lot of people die way too young. Years ago, they cried for many hours until the burial. Some would gash their legs, cut their hair, maybe even cut off the end of a finger if it was a husband or father or mother. We go to cemetery tomorrow for burial."

The following day was clear and cold. Late in the morning, a crowd of mourners gathered in the parking lot at the Sacajawea Cemetery. I put my hands deep into the pockets of my parka and stared at the gravel, listening to the keening of the women. The cemetery is on a hill, as laid out by the missionary Rev. John Roberts. Before Roberts came to Wind River, Shoshone were buried in various locations in mountain canyons. Roberts baptized many of the Shoshone and, after some years, his cemetery came to be the main burial place for the Shoshone tribe. Roberts named it after Sacajawea, the young Shoshone woman who accompanied the Lewis and Clark expedition.

A crier called out to us in Shoshone. His voice was loud enough to be heard over the women's keening. I picked out only some of the words: gather, to mourn, our brother. I guessed that the crier had also told us to accompany the casket on its journey up the hill because the crowd fell in line. Tom and I kept to the back of the crowd. We let the others move ahead up the hill.

At the grave site, the casket was opened one last time. Prayers were offered in Shoshone and people crowded close to the casket. Family members placed flowers on Toby's body. Some touched him. Keening grew louder and the crowd moved back from the grave. The casket was closed for the last time and lowered into its final resting place.

Tom and I turned to go. "There will be a giveaway at the mission after the burial," the crier called in Shoshone.

8. The Shoshone Episcopal Mission parish house, formerly a school for girls, 1970.

Tom and I got in the car and sat quietly, waiting for the long line of cars to wend its way out of the cemetery. The Shoshone Episcopal mission was only a short distance away. I could see its grove of pines and cottonwoods. Behind the trees sat a large Victorian brick building that had housed the Shoshone Girl's School for many years. Lack of support had forced the school to close years before.

When Tom and I arrived a few moments after everyone else, Toby's relatives still stood at the doorway. "Toby was one of our best peyote men on the reservation," Tom told them. "I feel sorrow deep in my heart."

Inside, there were only a few tables where food had been laid out so most of us sat on the floor in a large circle. I looked up at the tall windows and guessed that the room must have been the old mission school's main dining room. We were served lunch and Tom was asked to say a prayer of thanks for the food.

After lunch, Toby's closest relatives brought in baskets filled with a variety of items. They set the baskets in the center of the room. From the baskets, they took out bolts of cloth and clothing. Each adult guest received cloth or something to wear. For the children, there were toys. This was a Shoshone tradition and is called a "giveaway" because gifts are given away by the family of the deceased to all the mourners. Everybody receives something. Tom and I both received a new Western shirt.

As we drove away, Tom said, "Toby found peace at last and was taken to be with Our Father in heaven."

The next day proved to be sunny and warm for December and, with the sunshine, the somber tone of the last few days began to lift. At breakfast, I asked Tom if he'd like to take a drive, maybe the thirty miles to Riverton, thinking that it might cheer us up. We also needed some groceries, and we could get them at the big supermarket in Riverton. If we were going to Riverton, we'd be going through Arapaho country.

"You want to meet a really good Arapaho Indian, Johnson?" Tom asked. "Let's see if Bill Shakespeare is home."

I knew who Tom meant. Bill Shakespeare was a well-known Arapaho elder and a little bit glamorous because of his Hollywood connections. He might have been in an old Tim McCoy silent picture, *The Covered Wagon*, and Shakespeare and other Arapahos had accompanied McCoy to London in the 1920s. The Arapahos had pitched their teepees in a London park and attracted a lot of attention for their Wild West show.

"Sure I'd like to meet him," I said. "I've wanted to meet him for a long time. He was in show biz."

"He sure was. He's a good man, smart man, too, and he used to go into peyote meetings with some of us Shoshones. I saw him in town at the NuWay Café last summer. I give him a call, see if he's home," Tom said.

He walked over to the telephone, got out the phone book, and asked me to find the number. Tom could no longer see well enough to read the fine print in the phone book. Sure enough, William Shakespeare was listed. I read the number to Tom and he dialed it.

"Hello, Bill," Tom said now. "I'm your old friend Tom Wesaw. Say, I have a young anthropologist staying with me, learning Indian ways and the Shoshone language. Here he is. He wants to talk to you."

To my surprise, Tom handed me the phone. "Mr. Shakespeare?" I said.

"Sure, come on over," came the answer. His voice was strong. "I've got some stories to tell. I collect some of those old stories, stories the old people told us around the fire during the winter months. Winter is the time for telling stories."

On our drive, we passed by the Fort Washakie school. Tom looked over at it, a neat brick building about thirty or forty years old, and said, "I went to the old boarding school built long before this one. It's tore down now. It was a big building, had big mess hall. Always too hot or too cold. The teachers were strict, very strict. I didn't want to go—liked to work around my uncle's ranch. He had lots of cattle and horses and was a rich man. Even had a black hired man, but he made me go to school and said I had to learn to read and write English. Seemed like we kids all caught every cold or flu that came along. They made us cut our hair, take baths, and speak nothing but English. Of course we all spoke Shoshone out on the playground but we were put in the dunce seat if we talked Shoshone in the school. They taught us to pray at mealtime, too, but I already learned to pray from my uncle. I sure did learn to read and write but don't remember learning much else. I couldn't wait till my Uncle Bishop said I didn't have to go to school no more."

We drove on down the road toward Ethete. For a moment, my gaze left the road to follow the line of hills in the distance.

"*Heeto* is gone," Tom said.

"Who is gone?" I asked.

"A songbird, Johnson. You call it meadowlark. All the songbirds that used to sing are all gone."

Just past the school, we crossed over a large irrigation ditch.

"They call this the Coolidge canal," Tom said. "The Shoshone allotments were all on this side of it, the Arapaho allotments on the other side. That's the dividing line between the two tribes."

We passed the new Catholic mission church built out of cinder blocks and decorated with Arapaho geometric designs. Ethete was just a crossroads and Tom told me it meant "good" in Arapaho. "When I was young," he said, "the Arapahos had a big encampment here. They all lived in tents here."

We turned south, passing Shorty's gas station and another mission complex, this one called St. Michael's Episcopal Mission. We followed the winding, black-topped road east again past clusters of Arapaho homesteads toward St. Stephens Catholic Mission.

Bill Shakespeare lived on a ranch near St. Stephens, a good 20 miles east of Tom's place. Two houses sat on the Shakespeare property: one, a large log cabin, and the other, a small frame house where a tall, thin man stood in the doorway. That was Bill Shakespeare.

Inside his house, there seemed to be only one room with a table and chairs and a bed. We sat at the table and Bill poured us coffee.

"You know, Johnson always has questions," Tom said.

Bill smiled. "I've always had a lot of questions, too. Let's hear yours."

I said, "Bill, can you tell us how you came to be called Bill Shakespeare?"

He smiled. "The government agents came to the Indians years ago and told us that if we didn't have a white man's name, we needed to have one. We all had good Arapaho names, but they wanted to be able to keep records, and couldn't pronounce or spell very well those Arapaho words. They needed a first and a last name. So we all ended up with a white man's translation of our Arapaho name as a last name—like Yellow Bear, Sage, or even one like Wallowing Bull. The government couldn't translate very well. Some of the names didn't translate at all, and people didn't want them if they didn't, so my dad took the name of William Shakespeare because the agent told him it was a very distinguished name of a great English writer. Then when I came along, my dad named me William, too, but I've always been called Bill. Of course, I have an Arapaho name, too. When I went to boarding school I had a chance to read some Shakespeare and realized I had a good name, and was very proud to have it so I kept it. Some of our names come from other tribes or white men who married Arapaho women years ago, like Trosper or Felter."

Tom nodded. "Some of our Shoshone last names were given out in the same way as yours, Bill. My dad and uncles told the agent we already had a last name, but others like another uncle on my mother's side, Rabbittail, were translations of their Shoshone names. So my Aunt Mary, whose husband was Rabbittail, took that name as her last name. Wesaw was my dad's family name from long ago so we already had a last name. My son Delmar, the preacher, said he'd been preaching in Indiana and came across the name of a town called Wesaw, Indiana. He wondered if it came from a tribe that lived in Indiana at one time. Maybe, somehow, that name came out to Wyoming. Most of my people was from some different tribe, not Shoshone. My mother was *Datasiva*, Flathead, you know, and her grandfather, Iroquois. But we was all put on the rolls as Shoshone. My given name is Alessandro Wesaw but everybody calls me Tom."

A niece of Tom's had told me he had a Shoshone name. It was *Aa sugupë*, meaning Old Man Crow, on account of his trademark black Stetson.

"I knew a couple of your uncles on your mother's side," Bill said. "They were Flathead and they could speak Shoshone but we always talked in Indian sign language and could swap stories that way."

"You collect stories?" I asked.

"I have written down and recorded some of the old Arapaho stories told to me by elders back around World War I. Most of us lived in army tents or one-room log cabins in those days. During the long winter nights we kids listened to those stories around the campfire. It was really nice and warm in those tents. But they don't do that anymore, don't tell those stories. That's why I write them down and record them, so my grandchildren can hear them. I also tape-record songs, go around and some of the elders sing songs for me. I guess you could say I'm an anthropologist of my own people."

"That's what we should do among the Shoshones," Tom said. "You are a smart man, Bill Shakespeare. Say, do you remember the good times we used to have years ago?"

"Sure do," Bill said. "Now everything's about money, money, money. In those days, the government butchered cattle for us, and we had rations of bacon, flour, coffee. People stayed at home, grew gardens, raised cattle, told stories to educate their kids, didn't run off to town for every blessed thing.

Our people the Arapahos knew their stories, spoke their language all the time. In those days, when a young couple married, they stayed married and were watched by their parents. Of course, you might say that marriages were arranged, so both sets of parents knew what to expect."

"You are right," Tom said. "That's the way it was with Shoshone, too. There were some things about the old days I don't want to remember, too. Horses were better than cars in those days, 'cause the roads were so bad. If you had a car, when you ran out of gas, you might have to walk a long way to get some more. All we had was wagons to bring in freight. I used to help freight to Rawlins before the railroad came to Lander. That was a long road to go on. Now the roads are better and we travel faster. We just drive down to Rawlins in maybe three hours, not a whole day. We never got any payments from the tribe in those days, no oil or gas money, so we always needed cash. Old Matt McGuire ran the general store, and he gave you credit on things if you didn't have the money, but he always charged a lot. Now when we go to town to buy something, we don't pay so much. When we was young, everything was easier just because we was young. But sometimes we had lots of sickness, and many of us died, kids especially. Shoshones and Arapahos, too, right, Bill? Almost nobody lived as long in those days. Just a few lived to be over eighty, like me."

"You're right on that one, Tom. And I remember Arapaho Sun Dance time very well," said Bill. "All us kids had a great time going around to all the different camps. We could hear the drums from Ethete all the way down here, and those drums kept repeating in my ears. They had a good message, saying, *Your people are gathered here to make good medicine for you.*"

"I hope I can visit both the Shoshone and the Arapaho Sun Dances next summer," I said. "Bill, I wanted to ask you about the time all those younger Arapaho went to London back in the 1920s. Did you go?"

"I sure did," Bill said. "And did you hear about Tim McCoy? He starred in lots of Hollywood movies. He might be still living. Tim worked around here at the old Em-Bar ranch, and later he had a ranch of his own in the Owl Creek Mountains. He knew a lot of the old timers, like Sage and my dad, War Bonnet, and they liked him 'cause he respected Indian ways. McCoy's the one got the idea of taking a Wild West show to London, England. Even took Arapaho to California, camping out in one of those canyons and made a movie, acting just like the Indians used to, riding horses, on the warpath, hunting buffalo, and all that."

"I remember that well," Tom said.

"I don't know if Tim McCoy is still living, but if he is, he'd be older than me," Bill said. "He'd be in his eighties by now. London was a real adventure. Of course, most of us younger men, those who had been to boarding school here at St. Stephens or one of the other boarding schools like Genoa or Haskell, studied geography and we knew London was the capital of England and a very big and old city. For us, this was the chance of a lifetime to travel. When Tim and the other guys told us we could play like we were the 'wild Indians' of the movies, Indians who went to war, painted their faces, sang war songs, and held dances, we decided he could ham it up. We weren't like that. It was just a fiction, you know, just a story. If we had been left alone to live in peace, we'd be what we always were before the whites came and took our country, but the whites had this idea that we should play like we are savages, wild and warlike all the time. Some of us didn't like it, but we were young and decided to go along with it. I was just as restless as the other young men in those days."

"What did you think of London?" I asked.

"Well, that was some place," he said. "When the rain set in, we were put up in a big boarding house and the lady who was in charge didn't like us at all. She called us a bunch of thievin' savages. So we didn't like her, either, and I guess you could say we weren't all that respectful toward her. We just hammed it up, had a good time and I think probably drank too much, too. The English liked our shows but, you know, I wanted to tell the newspapers that this show wasn't anything like what we really are."

"I was just like you," Tom said. "I liked to travel. I went over to Montana to visit Flathead relatives and down to Idaho many times."

I said, "I suppose the Wild West was still in the mind of the English, even in the 1920s, with wild Indians fighting cowboys and all that. The British had their own colonies in Africa and they had all been told stories about how the Africans lived and how they acted like savages. I'm not surprised if they wanted to believe the same things about American Indians. Of course, it's not true that the Africans were savages and it's not true that Indians were, either."

Tom gave a deep nod. "Wyoming is really different now than it was when I was a young man. We had lots of rustlers and horse thieves who hid out back in the canyons, and the law couldn't get them. They stole from us Indians, too." To Bill he said, "You Arapaho all got back home safely, didn't you?"

"Sure did," Bill said with a note of satisfaction. "Say, do you want to listen to a tape I have of some Indian music?"

Tom and I looked at each other and we both said, "Sure."

Bill reached for a shelf where he kept his tapes, placed one in what looked to be a new Sony recorder, and said, "I taped this at last year's Sun Dance."

We listened to the entire tape, sitting there, drinking our coffee. When it was finished, Tom said, "That song reminds me of our Sun Dance. I always let Arapahos dance in our Sun Dance. Theirs is different from ours but we all pray to the same God."

7

POLITICS

It was what Tom called an "open winter" in Wyoming, a winter with little snow in the Wind River valley. This made it easy to move about. We continued our drives around the reservation and to Lander. Day after day in January, the sky was a clean, clear blue, and a flannel shirt under my parka and a pair of thick socks in my boots were enough to keep me warm.

One Saturday, Tom and I went to a peyote meeting at the home of a relative. In the warmth of the peyote teepee after the meeting, the talk drifted to the Shoshone Business Council. Two of the men at the meeting were members.

"We're talking about enrollment again in the council tomorrow morning," one of the men said, lowering his voice to a confidential murmur. "One of my cousins keeps wanting to enroll his daughter. We've tabled the enrollment twice and he's come back to us again demanding that she be enrolled. He says the last council approved the enrollment of some kids who were less than one-quarter Shoshone blood, so we'd better enroll her, too. She's three-sixteenths. Trouble is, if we enroll her, the word'll get out and we'll open the door for more people who insist on getting children or grandchildren enrolled."

Day in and day out, it seemed, I was hearing about enrollment, meaning membership in the tribe. The talk, bound to raise a lot of anger, had to do with the U.S. government's long imposition of who could and could not be an official member of any recognized tribe. It also had to do with the plain fact that logic didn't always appear to be the federal government's strong suit. As soon as the treaties with the Eastern Shoshone were made in the nineteenth century, the U.S. government drew up a list of everybody who was deemed to be a member of the tribe. Some of the people on that list were actually born into other tribes or had married into the tribe. Some were of mixed Indian ancestry; others were part European American or Mexican or African American. The United States did not have deep knowledge or expertise about who should have been included on the tribal roll and who should not. What defined the tribe as Shoshone was a core of people who spoke the Shoshone language and lived together, but beyond that, the parameters of who could be included in tribal membership were pretty broad. Not only did it include some who had married into the tribe recently but there also were some who were really Comanche or Ute who had been accepted into the tribe years before. Some were probably refugees from tribes to the east and sought freedom among the Shoshone before white settlement caught up to them. Even Washakie, held by the U.S. government to be the chief of the Eastern Shoshones, is said to have been Flathead on his mother's side and Umatilla on his father's. How much actual Shoshone ancestry he had may never be known.

Until at least the 1930s, the United States government advised that in order to be a member of a certain tribe, you had to have the equivalent of at least one grandparent in ancestry, or one-quarter Shoshone, for example, to be enrolled. Ancestry was always phrased in terms of "blood." From the government's point of view—not necessarily the tribe's—limits had to be placed and it's doubtful whether cultural knowledge or what tribe you were born into had anything to do with the way the United States reasoned. It had to do with land. If all descendants of a tribe could claim membership, the amount of land that needed to be reserved for future generations might expand. The government wanted to reserve as little land as possible out of the entire country for Indians. The United States wanted its territory as free as possible for European settlement and Indians had been deliberately displaced. So, the government laid down strict rules. It strongly suggested that one-quarter "blood" should be the minimum for enrollment in a federally recognized tribe.

Most tribal members were held to be wards of the government until 1924 when the United States finally granted them all citizenship. The Indian Reorganization Act of 1934 gave the tribes greater autonomy in determining their enrollment regulation. This means that requirement for tribal membership could vary from the government's one-quarter blood requirement if tribes wanted to alter their enrollment regulations. As of this writing, tribal enrollment regulations run the gamut from very open—anyone descended from a person on certain nineteenth-century rolls with no importance given to percentage of Indian ancestry—to more restrictive, like the one-quarter plus DNA testing required by the Ho Chunk nation of Wisconsin. Many tribes still follow the one-quarter "blood" percentage rule and continue to use "blood" or ancestry as the criterion.

In the peyote teepee that morning, there was anger and the occasional raised voice. How many other groups in the United States spend any time thinking about how much ancestry is required to belong to the group they were born into?

"A rule is a rule," a woman said.

"No, rules are made to be broken," another countered.

"No, you got that wrong," said a third. "A rule is made to be broken only if you've got pull."

The conversation went on like this until Tom spoke. Everyone in the teepee turned to him. "There's always been a big fight about enrollment," he said. "Even when I was young man, the full-bloods kept wanting to keep the breeds out. Kept saying they wasn't real Shoshones. There was a lot of breeds in our tribe, so as time went by the full-bloods were outnumbered. After the government let us make our own enrollment rules, the full-bloods wanted to keep the one-quarter rule and were always saying that if you was less than that chances are you didn't speak or act like a Shoshone, didn't come to our dances and events, neither. I always took the side of the full-blood Shoshones 'cause my wife, Helen, was one but I was a breed myself—part French and Iroquois and Flathead, and I don't know how much Shoshone from way back. That daughter you're talking about whose dad wants her to be enrolled is a relative of mine. His father was Flathead and Iroquois but when the whole family came down to settle here at the invitation of old Chief Washakie, their uncle, they were put on the Shoshone rolls. There wasn't no other place to put them and they lived here. Then there was a whole family of Sioux who came to Chief Washakie about the same time looking for safety from that group of Sioux that hated the government. Washakie was at peace with the government by that time, so he let them stay, and they got on the rolls. There was Comanche, Utes, and Western Shoshone who came in, too. Some Shoshones married Mexicans. So from the start of this reservation there was always other tribes intermixed with the Shoshone, and whites, too."

Heads were nodding. I asked, "If the government put people who lived with the Shoshone from other tribal backgrounds on the original rolls, couldn't the tribe do the same thing today?"

"It's a real touchy issue," a man next to me said. "Some people think the tribe's big enough already and some think it's too small. There's people who want to keep the enrollment down so the tribe's income will be spread out among less people and those people will get more income. Then, there's those that live in Lander or Riverton, or maybe even Casper who don't live on the reservation at all but still want the medical and dental services from Indian Health. Their children usually get those things, anyway, even if they're not enrolled, but some of them drive a long distance to get them, and they want their kids to be enrolled. I know someone who drives from Las Vegas for free dental work for her kids. Then there's people married into the tribe just like some of us who want to be part of the Shoshone tribe because we are Indian and like to practice Indian ways. Some of them don't have enough Shoshone ancestry to be enrolled but they live here and raise their kids here. In the old days before there were government rolls of who was or who wasn't Shoshone, all those kids would have been part of the tribe, no questions asked. Washakie would have allowed them all in."

"We shouldn't even have to talk about this," said Tom. "Whites don't have to worry if they're part English or German to be citizens of the United States. Our old chief, my grandfather Washakie, would have let them on the rolls if they lived here. Remember, his last wife, Aawaipe, was Crow and Charlie, our best peyote leader, was their son."

One of Tom's relatives sitting on the other side of the teepee said, "I know I tried to get my daughter enrolled last year and she couldn't qualify because her dad's a full-blood Arapaho and I'm three-eighths Shoshone. They told me her dad's blood wouldn't help her get enrolled as a Shoshone because she should get enrolled as an Arapaho. The Arapahos only allow the children whose father is Arapaho to be enrolled and even if I tried to get her enrolled Shoshone, she couldn't add in her dad's blood so she couldn't get enrolled 'cause she'd only be three-sixteenths Shoshone and she'd lose all her dad's Arapaho blood. None of it's fair. We live here and have always lived here. These are my people and I consider them my tribe and my people whether they're enrolled or not. So why should my daughter be punished?"

One woman said the government should have been strict from the start and never let people from other tribes on the rolls. Even half-breeds, she said, should have been excluded. "That's where all this mess started," she said.

Another woman looked straight at her and said, "If that had happened, our tribe would be so small today and only those few would get all the oil and gas money that rightfully belongs to all of us whose old people settled here."

"It's just like Tom said," another man put in. "The government did this to us, and now we have to figure out who's Shoshone or who isn't if we want to be Indian. Most of those who say they're full blood have kids or grandkids who married someone from a different tribe or even whites. Some day the Shoshone blood in them will be so small that it won't even count. I say everybody should be given all the rights to our land and the money we get if their families always lived here."

Conversation turned to other things, and after dinner Tom and I drove home. As we passed the general store, Tom said, "We've always had folks from different tribes who got enrolled years ago and now they're all Shoshone. They speak our language, live here, be in Sun Dance and peyote, everything. It don't matter what your grandfather's tribe was if you live here, come to meetings, dances, events. Back in the early days, even when I was young, there was kids adopted into the tribe and we didn't know who their parents were. It didn't matter either as long as they lived here, went to school and went to dances and such. Today we're all mixed up but being Shoshone still means being in Sun Dance, in peyote meetings, going to Indian Days. You go to council meetings, Johnson. You can find out for yourself what's happening and let us know about it."

By *us*, I assumed Tom meant his friends and relatives. "Sure, I'll go," I said. "The meetings are open, aren't they?"

"Other people go so you can, too," Tom said.

The next morning, I was at the tribal offices in Fort Washakie a good fifteen minutes before the business council was to meet. Some of the six council members knew who I was and greeted me. The meeting room had theater seats; I took one toward the back. I expected them to fill but I remained the only member of the audience. Everyone else was a council member. One, a woman I already knew from the motel she ran by the highway, made the motion that all grandchildren of any person already enrolled could be enrolled, regardless of their blood percentage.

The motion didn't surprise me. I had suspected there would be a reaction to what I'd heard at the peyote meeting about the business council's vote to enroll grandchildren who were less than one-quarter Shoshone. The motel owner was angry. She lifted her chin and threatened to take her motion to the next meeting of the general council, which is the council of the whole tribe where all enrollments have to be approved. The general council could fail to act on a recommendation to enroll passed by the business council, she reminded us. She waited a moment but there was no reaction.

"I'll make a motion that any and all grandchildren of any enrolled member can be enrolled, regardless of ancestry," she said.

The others, all men, shifted uneasily in their seats. One said, "Now, c'mon."

"If so-and-so can get his grandkids on, then so can I!" she almost shouted. "Only the general council has the power to change enrollment regulations. You all know that. This business council tried to sneak things through."

I reported these events back to Tom. He said there'd be a big show-down at the meeting of the general council in February. In the meantime, we had to get going to another peyote meeting, he said. This meeting was going to be a happy event. It was to be a celebration of a little girl's birthday. The family lived in a nice trailer house up near Kinnear.

"Let's ghost," Tom said.

The drive to Kinnear took twenty minutes or so. As we passed the settlement of Shoshone at Sage Creek, Tom said, "This is where a lot of the old-time Mountain Shoshone live."

"We haven't been to visit them," I said.

"That's right," Tom said. "They have their own doctor. All my relatives live on Trout Creek and around the Fort."

The peyote ceremony for the little girl's meeting was attended by close friends and relatives and everybody made over her. Tom brushed her with eagle feathers and gave her sweets after the meeting was over. As we sat around the fire talking in the morning hours, the issue of enrollment came up again. People were talking about it all the time in those days. The little girl's father was enrolled in Montana and had no Shoshone ancestry. They could not add in his Crow ancestry because it was not Shoshone.

"That's what really makes me mad," the girl's mother said. "We can't count any of my husband's Indian blood so our kid ends up losing some of her ancestry. It's stupid and for what reason? None. They just want to squeeze us off the rolls. Pretty soon we won't have a Shoshone tribe anymore."

Tom and I talked about this more as we drove back from the peyote meeting. "It's always been a big problem and only gets worse," he said.

Toward the end of February, a general council meeting was called. This time, Tom went with me. The general council met in the large auditorium of Rocky Mountain Hall. Several hundred people packed the place. Things had heated up. As promised, the motel owner made her motion that all grandchildren of any enrolled person could be enrolled, regardless of their percentage of Shoshone blood.

The discussion was orderly. One by one, people came to the microphone. Some agreed with the motion and argued that it would open the tribe's rolls. The tribe was getting too small, they said, and many children were being denied enrollment. Children needed the advantages of tribal membership, they said. Others were adamantly opposed. There had to be limits, they said, and if a grandparent was only one-quarter Shoshone, some grandchildren might only be one-sixteenth Shoshone and that would simply be going too far.

Finally, a woman stood, and Tom elbowed me to pay attention. "I am part Arapaho and white, besides being an enrolled Shoshone," she said. "If we don't open up the rolls farther, the tribe will simply get smaller and smaller. Worse yet, those children who don't qualify will live here but have nothing to do with the business of the tribe or receive any income from it. There are already hundreds of nonenrolled children living on the reservation. It isn't fair that all these children of mixed tribal and other backgrounds not be on the rolls. Our chief would have wanted this. He would have wanted them on the rolls."

Tom leaned over and whispered in my ear, "She's right."

A man in front of us stood up. "One-sixteenth is such a small percentage of Shoshone ancestry. The ones that would get on the rolls from this might be people who never live in Wyoming or on the reservation. How Indian will those kids be?"

A murmur of agreement rippled through the audience. "We have to set a limit, a boundary for what entitles you to be a member of this tribe," a man said.

A prominent elder got up to speak. "I move we change the enrollment regulations from one-quarter to anybody who is at least one-eighth Shoshone. If you are one-eighth Shoshone you will be accepted for enrollment."

Someone sitting next to him seconded it. People turned toward each other and spoke in low tones. Tom looked at me and I at him. "I didn't expect that one, but I guess I can vote yes on it," he said. "That'll take care of all the anger about enrolling grandchildren who were just a little less than one-quarter. At the same time, those who are only one-sixteenth can't get enrolled."

An amendment was proposed to the motion. It stated that, in order to be enrolled, any person less than one-quarter Shoshone had to live in the county that included the reservation. The sponsor said that his idea was to make sure these new tribal members were part of the community and could be around for meetings and events.

It sounded like a good idea to me but the amendment died for lack of a second. On further thought, I realized that many people had grandchildren in the armed services or relatives who lived with other tribes or in distant places, far from Fremont County.

The vote on the motion was called by voice, yea or nay. The yeas and nays were so even that a second vote was needed, this time by hand instead of voice. The motion was read once again, that anyone who was descended from a tribal member and was at least one-eighth Shoshone was eligible for enrollment.

Tom's hand went up in favor.

"A lot of people are really mad about this," Tom said low. "This isn't the end of the story. It's a big mess, just like it always has been and always will be. The government did this to us and we're still letting them do it to us by fighting each other. Our Indian way is to work together, not to fight each other."

The motion passed by a slim margin. I took Tom home and decided to find out more about the other big problem that the government had created, the inheritance of land on the reservation.

I already had some background on the allotment era and its problems. Back in 1887, the Dawes Severalty, or General Allotment Act, was passed. It started a massive effort to give each American Indian family an allotment, a piece of land of several hundred acres out of land already reserved to them by treaty. The amount of land depended on the size of the family. Allotment was resisted at Wind River because very little land was irrigated and therefore not fit for cultivation. Eventually, reservoirs were built and irrigation canals brought water from the mountains to the valley. The original families that were given allotments multiplied. By 1970 there were more than twice as many Shoshone and even more than twice as many Arapaho as during the allotment period seventy years earlier. Parcels of land were rented out, sold, and fragmented. Sometimes there were dozens of heirs for one allotment of a little more than one hundred acres. That land, rented out, brought in only a few dollars to each heir, and created a huge amount of work for Bureau of Indian Affairs employees.

Usually, wealthier non-Indian ranchers ended up renting the land. There were only a few allotments that were still being worked by descendants of those originally given the land. I drove back to the Fort and parked my car at the agency. I was lucky: the man I wanted to see at the Bureau of Indian Affairs was in. As I was ushered into Mr. Steinwand's office, I asked, "How successful are the efforts to get the heirs to consolidate holdings?" I asked.

"Not good at all," Steinwand said. "People can't get together and there's too much bickering. They can't agree on a fair price and really don't want the land sold out of the tribe. They don't want to lose the right to the land but in most cases people don't have the capital to run a ranch and they don't have the money to buy out other heirs. They're caught between a rock and a hard place. Too bad the tribe couldn't have bought some of these holdings and made them into a kind of Shoshone ranch that was owned and operated by the tribe. So we're left with dozens, maybe hundreds, of heirs to a small ranch who rent it out to a non-Indian, and collect maybe only a few dollars per year in rents. It's a mess."

When I reported back to Tom on my discussion with Mr. Steinwand, he shook his head slowly. "I get some money for renting out my pasture and from the bee man that collects honey from my hives," he said. "It pays my phone and electric bills. That money goes in with the per capita from the tribe. It's enough for me to live on. I know why some people want to keep our tribe small but our old people, the people who taught me when I was a kid, they would never agree to that."

THE SWEAT SOLUTION

THE SHOSHONE CALL THE WIND RIVER VALLEY WARM VALLEY, AND IT IS
said that Washakie chose it as a place for the Shoshone to live for its rela-
tively moderate weather. By March of my stay with Tom, not very much
snow had fallen in the valley and, in the areas that were not shaded, most
of it had melted. Behind Tom's house, the mountains were shrouded in
snow and got a new dusting of it every week or so. The whiteness of the
snowy mountains against the blue sky stood in sharp contrast with the
valley. In the valley, everything was still brown, and Tom said it would be
another month or more before the willows would green up.

One Monday morning the weather was so clear that Tom told me that
he was going to put up a sweat later that week. The weather looked to him
like it would hold. The sweat was going to be for Sam Timbe. I had seen
Sam—early twenties, friendly guy—at peyote meetings several times and
over at the Sacajawea Service Station where he worked. Sam's family lived
a couple of hundred yards farther up Trout Creek Road from Tom's, and
his dad always had plenty of alfalfa hay from his irrigated fields.

Sam had married one of Tom's distant relatives a couple of years ago.
Tom called her his niece. The girl's name was Rose; she had graduated
from one of the best government-sponsored schools for Indian students,
the Haskell Indian Nations University in Lawrence, Kansas. Now Rose
worked as a secretary for the tribe and she had ambitions for Sam: she
wanted him to open his own business. He should become a mechanic so
he could start his own business repairing cars and trucks, she thought.
To get the training, Sam would need to go to the technical college in
Casper.

Tom poured himself a second mug of morning coffee. "Sam wants me
to put up a sweat here to pray for good things to happen so he don't have
to go to school," he said gravely. "He's not happy about leaving the reservation. He just wants to stay by his dad, working on the ranch and working

part-time at the service station. Besides, his dad's getting on in years and needs someone to take over the ranch. Trouble is, Rose says unless he goes on to have a good job as mechanic, she won't stay with him."

I was about to ask why Tom didn't just have a talk with Rose if her plan was so bad, but thought better of it. Instead I asked, "Do they have any kids?"

Tom pursed his lips and sadly shook his head. "Not yet. That's another part of the mix-up," he said. "Sam wants to have kids and his wife wants him to get training in mechanics first and set up business so they can build a new house and live down at the Fort. They have lots of fights at home and Sam doesn't like all that. Back in the days before cars, we never worried about what you'd do with your life after you got married. Me, I had allotment next to land my uncle had here on Trout Creek. I didn't want to be a farmer, so when the agency opened their own flour mill I applied for the job and got it. By then, I already had a couple of kids. I leased out some of the land and still do and retired from the mill when I could. I went around to Shoshone people doctoring, leading sweats and Sun Dances and peyote meetings, and that was what I really wanted to do, help my people. There was lots of sickness in those days, too, and they really needed me. I never had to wonder about whether I should leave or get more education or what."

Since the enrollment dustup, I had gotten into the habit of going to various committee meetings. They were better than any newspaper for keeping up. "I hear a lot of talk about taking up vocational training at council meetings," I said. "They have programs now to send young people to the cities for vocational training. The government pays their expenses. You can go to Casper or Denver or Salt Lake and learn all kinds of things and there are good jobs waiting for you there."

"That's been true for years. Lots of Shoshone and Arapaho kids go away to the cities for a while but most of them come back. We'll have that sweat for Sam and maybe help him work out those problems," Tom said.

"I'll help split the wood for the fire and get the rocks and everything else ready. When does he want to have the sweat?" I asked.

"Saturday afternoon, if it isn't too cold," Tom said.

The next day, in Lander, Tom and I headed for lunch at the NuWay Café. Coming out as we were going in was another of Tom's nieces, Marisa. Marisa greeted us with a smile and a wave of her hand and said, "Hi Two Toms. What's up? How are you bachelors getting along?"

"Oh, just doing a few errands and getting some supplies," Tom said. "How you doing?"

"I've almost given up on Al," she said. "I thought maybe he'd help make some beef jerky for us for the winter, like my mom and dad used to do, but he'd rather be up on Black Mountain hunting elk. 'Course, the meat we get is really good, but I could use more help down at the ranch house sometimes, too. Making jerky is hard work. You have to cut all the meat into strips and dry it outside. Otherwise, we get along pretty good. It's a long drive down to the Fort from Crowheart. I don't know, maybe I should quit and stay home instead of running a kindergarten for other people's kids. I don't know."

The moment the two of us were seated, Tom said, "Marisa and Al wanted to have kids but she don't have any and they've been married a long time. I think they want to adopt some foster kids, Shoshone kids. Marisa asked me to pray for her several times. She wants to have children and thought that my prayers would help. I've treated women before. Sometimes they start having kids. It's kind of like a miracle. God is the power behind it."

The next day, two cousins of Sam's drove up to Tom's place and offered to help split wood for the sweat. They were planning to be at the sweat on Saturday morning, they said. As we split up the wood and moved the volcanic rocks into place, the older of the two said that Sam had been having bad dreams, dreams that his wife Rose might leave him. Maybe prayers could help, he said.

"I'm sure glad you are coming to help us out on Saturday," I said. "Tommy Wesaw will be there, too. Sam. You two. Old Tom and me. That's six. No, seven with Al."

"Tommy's like an uncle to me," said the younger man. "He's a good mechanic, too. Always stayed around his dad's place. Finally married a couple of years ago."

Thursday, Tom and I went out to visit old friends of his, Harry and Hugo Bonatsie. They didn't have a phone but Tom had seen them down at Rocky Mountain Hall recently. Their knees bothered them and they asked Tom to stop by when he had the time. Tom always brought his peyote box with him when he visited the Bonatsies. Today, he also had a tube of Ben Gay ointment with him.

"Roll up your pants," he told them. "This medicine will help you." Tom followed up the Ben Gay with his eagle fans and prayer. Then the three of

9. Ranch house of Susie Ward near Sage Creek, 1969.

them reminisced about the old days when everything was done with horses and the horse you had was your most important possession.

Friday, we went out to visit Susie Ward on her ranch a few miles from the Fort. This visit was strictly social. Tom had never doctored Susie, he had told me, because she had never asked. They were old friends and family by marriage: Susie was the grandmother of the husband of one of Tom's granddaughters. She was in her nineties but still very alert. Her parents were "breed Sioux," originally from the Dakotas and allied with the United States during the Fort Fetterman massacre. They had found refuge on the Wind River Reservation. Her husband, Dell, had been dead for a number of years. He was a white man, a pioneer, and had built the ranch where they lived on Sage Creek. Her house, straight out of the 1880s, was built of logs.

Tom rapped on the door and Susie let us in. She was very old, no doubt about that, but her powdered face, her quick nods, and her eyes, clear and lively behind cat-eye glasses frames, gave away her spryness. She held a phonebook. "Come in!" she said. "Sit down! Oh, and let me put down this phonebook! I can get back to that at any time!"

She set the phonebook on the shelf of a whatnot that also held her phone and I took a look around the front room. Its log walls and low ceiling were painted white and the floor was linoleum with braided rugs. The two small windows were squeaky clean. There were a couple of Victorian rockers, a horsehair sofa, and a cast-iron stove.

"We was over by the Fort so we thought we'd stop by," Tom said.

"Tom, you and I remember how different the Fort was when the army was stationed there. Oh, the Fort is so different than it was when we were young!" Susie said. "When the army was stationed down at the Fort, young people from all over used to attend those dances, and some of those social events led to marriage."

"Now everybody has cars and can go into town and go to the bars. That's where a lot of the trouble begins," Tom said.

"We didn't have much money but we sure had fun!" Susie said. "Today it's all about money, money, money."

Tom nodded. "The Indians are forgetting the old ways. That's what kept us in line. The old men would lecture us, over and over, and we had to obey them. Today, most parents really care, but they can't stop the young folks from doin' pretty much what they want to. Your husband was one of those good white men—*zan dan taivo*. There was plenty of whites that wasn't so good, too, but they all left the reservation after they cheated someone in poker, stole some money, or got in fights. Dell stayed and raised a family. I've been teaching young Tom here all those good things, Indian ways."

"That's good!" Susie said. "My folks were Sioux and French but Chief Washakie welcomed us and my folks. He thought Dell was a good man, like you think, Tom. Nobody objected to him living here. He was a hard worker and I was proud of him."

"That's right. You all came here long ago and are a credit to the tribe. Any of your grandkids should be enrolled, too. There's a big squabble going on about that now. You've been part of the tribe ever since your folks came here, long before I was born. Your kids and grandkids are part of the tribe. They carry on the Shoshone ways just like anyone else," Tom said.

"Oh, that enrollment mess!" Susie said. "The full-bloods are always saying that the only real Shoshone is a full-blood Shoshone. Trouble is, there just aren't very many of those left!"

"We've got to work together as a tribe. We're all part of this tribe together, full-bloods and breeds," Tom said. "I want Johnson to know this. I want him to take all this down because I'm old. You're old, Susie. Soon we won't be here. Johnson can write this for everyone to know."

After we got home, we went out to the sweat area just north of his house to see that all the wood was stacked neatly and waiting for the next day's ceremony. We had already covered the sweat lodge with a new canvas. Everything was ready.

Saturday morning dawned bright and clear. The temperature might climb into the fifties by midafternoon. It was going to be a perfect day for a sweat.

Sam's two cousins who had helped me chop the wood were the first to drive up Tom's lane. They waved and parked their pickup, got out, and went over to the sweat lodge. A few minutes later, Sam arrived. Tommy Wesaw walked across the alfalfa field from his place. He was going to be the fireman for this sweat. Then Al from up near Crowheart appeared. Together with Tom and myself, there would be seven of us for the sweat.

Tommy dashed some kerosene over the logs and threw a match into it. The flames blazed. We stood around waiting for them to burn down so we could move some hot rocks into the sweat lodge. After about twenty or thirty minutes, the wood had burned down to mostly embers. The volcanic rocks glowed red-hot. Tommy had a shovel ready and began moving them into the pit in the center of the sweat lodge. We took off our heavy pants and shirts, down to our shorts, and crawled into the sweat lodge, leaving our clothes behind. Tommy entered last and closed the flap.

"*Dam Apë*, hear us," Tom prayed. "We ask you to take pity on us. We are only humble men, people, and ask you to listen to us."

Each one of the men offered prayers, and Tom splashed water on the hot rocks. Steam rose up. The men prayed for help and an answer to what they had experienced in their dreams. Those dreams had been about painful things, they said, disagreements between them and their family. They asked that *Dam Apë* give them blessings and send them help.

Tom splashed more water on the hot rocks. After two rounds of prayers and sweating, we got out and stood around the remains of the fire, rubbing ourselves with towels. One of the cousins said, "Sam, I know that Pete and I can help you with the ranch if you want to go to Casper for that training."

Al nodded. "Marisa comes down to the Fort every day," he said. "She and Rose can visit with each other. Maybe Rose can move in with her parents if you go to Casper. You'll be back on weekends and that'll help. I'll just bet that the business council can help pay for your training in Casper."

Sam did not answer. He pushed at the dirt with his foot. Then, after pursing his lips in thought, he said, "I'd really like to get more training and open my own business, but you know, Dad does need help and I can't spread myself too thin."

"I can get some more help from a couple of guys I know who are fire-fighters but don't have work all the time, especially in winter," Al said.

One of the cousins added another thought. "It's really rough in the summer around Sun Dance time when you have to cut and bail hay and that's when we can get a couple more guys together to help out. I know you can make it at Casper. You already know a lot about cars and trucks, inside-out."

"I'll have to think about it," Sam said.

We moved into the sweat lodge again for the remaining two rounds. The sweat was so relaxing, the thought crossed my mind that this kind of place would be the perfect environment for getting any two or three people together to increase understanding. It also struck me that these men believed that they needed other people. They expected to work with others to find solutions.

Tom offered a long closing prayer, the kind of prayer that asked *Dam Apë* for help and guidance. He said, "You good man, Sam, and Rose is a good wife. You two stick together and the rest of us will help you out."

"I'll have to talk to Rose tonight and work things out so she can keep her job while I go to Casper," Sam said. His eyes swept our faces. "Thanks everyone. Thanks for helping to clear my mind. I had so many bad dreams about Rose leaving me but I know things can work out now."

We put on our Levis and flannel shirts and moved over to the house to have some coffee. Everyone felt good and just before the men left, Tom offered another prayer. "*Dam Apë*, you have given us so much to be thankful for. Thank you for being with us in that sweat. So be it."

9

What I Learned from Tom

After a couple of late snows in April, the willows started budding. My grandmother who helped raise me was in poor health. I needed to go to her, which meant my time with Tom had to come to an end. Saying good-bye to Tom wasn't going to be easy.

Tom was always happiest when he was with young people. Just now, a teenage grandson of Tom's was staying with us. The grandson was not particularly interested in Indian ways. He liked rock 'n' roll and television and his plans as to how long he'd stay were unsure. Doreen, Tom's girlfriend from the fall months, had decided to take a retraining grant in Casper to learn accounting. When her dad told us about the grant at the close of a peyote meeting, he said he hoped she'd be able to find a job with the tribe or the Bureau of Indian Affairs.

To break the tension of my leaving, Tom and I decided to go into Lander. He wanted me to meet a relative of his who had just opened up a saddle shop on Main Street. Buddy Boller was in his thirties and just beginning to build a reputation as a Western artist. He sold beads and Indian beadwork as well as saddles and other leather goods. "I've heard good things about you, Tom," Buddy said to me, after he'd given us a tour of his shop. "You're taking good care of our grandpa here. I've got some nice Shoshone beadwork for sale if you'd like to look." Tom and I looked around the store and admired the tooled leather and saddle work. I bought some beads for Tom to give to his granddaughter Loreena, and some more for his friends.

We wished Buddy success in his business and left to have lunch. It was just before noon and the NuWay Café was already crowded. Daisy and Herman St. Clair from Wind River were sitting in one booth. Herman represented the Shoshone in many official functions and Daisy always looked nice. Today she was wearing one of her attractive dresses with wide sleeves. It was a cloth version of the beaded soft buckskin dresses worn many years ago.

"Hi, Two Toms," Daisy said with a smile.

I swallowed back a lump in my throat. That particular nickname, I would miss.

Tom and I moved down to the back of the café to the last remaining empty booth. We ordered "the usual"—a cheeseburger and fries for me and a hot beef dinner with mashed potatoes and gravy for Tom. Coffee.

Waiting for the coffee to come, I looked at the people sitting near us. A reporter for the local newspaper, Inez Osgood, was one table over. Inez wrote a column for the paper called "This 'n' That." She always ate in one of the cafés on Main Street for lunch and everybody knew her. If a person had some news or gossip to spread, then Inez was the person to see. Everybody in Lander and most of the Shoshone that I knew complained about her. "An old busybody," one said. "Makes everybody's own business hers," said another.

Today, Inez was in a more animated mood than usual. I looked at Tom; he was looking at me, eyebrows raised. He wanted to turn our ears up and our voices down.

"I heard the Shoshones are getting a raise in their per-capitas," Inez said to her friend. She must not have noticed Tom and me so close by.

"Oh, tell me more," said her companion.

"Well," said Inez, "the price of oil and gas is going up and we all have to pay for it but guess who's getting the benefit? The Indians, of course. They'll take advantage of that for sure. They're rich enough to hire lawyers, you know, and it's just coincidence that all that oil happened to be on their land."

"I wouldn't make a big fuss about it, Inez. The government gave them a big reservation. Wanted to pay off Washakie and hoped that by moving the Shoshone away from the main line of the railroad they'd get rid of them," her friend said. "With more money, the Indians will just spend it here in Lander, and it'll come back to us sooner or later. They've only got that one store on the reservation. Do most of their shopping in town, anyway. Some of the better ones even have bank accounts."

Inez furrowed her brow in a twinge of moral distress. "Well, to be honest with you, I never did think the Indians deserved all that revenue they get. Most of them can't save a nickel or they just drink it all up as soon as they get their check. And then they want to be recognized as the first people around here. Well, I've got news for some of them. There was whites in South Pass prospecting for gold before the Shoshones got their reservation and came here. The businesses in Lander got their start from that money earned in South Pass and that's what's made the community count for something, not the Indians."

My own mouth puckered with annoyance. I glanced at Tom: he had stiffened. I knew he didn't want to make a scene, that there was no point in making a scene with this particular person. Inez's conversation continued in the same vein until the waitress brought food to us. Inez happened to look over at our booth and recognized Tom. She changed the subject quickly, saying, "I wonder what old man Del Monte is going to do with the Noble Hotel. Heard he might sell it to that Petzoldt crowd that brings in rich folks from back east who want to use our mountains to teach wilderness survival. Won't help the ranchers much, will it?"

Tom and I bolted our food, got the bill, and left. We walked in silence to Joe's Place and I got Tom a new bolo tie as a parting gift and a couple of Western shirts with pearlized snap buttons to take along to Iowa. I told Joe I was going back to Iowa soon and didn't know when I'd be back.

It wasn't until Tom and I were on the road back to the reservation that Tom broached the subject of what we'd heard in the café. "Some whites are good people and treat Indians like they would anybody else," Tom said. "Some are just greedy. Some Indians are like that, too. Even when I was young man, there was always some like that. My uncle Bishop used to say, stay away from those people, white or Indian. They'll just cheat you. I never forgot what he said."

"To say that the Indians don't deserve more money for their oil and gas on their own land says a lot about what these people think," I blurted. The words fizzed out of me like from a shaken up soda pop bottle with its cap finally off. "All they wanted was for Indians to starve or die, just go away, never getting anything back from this whole country that was theirs to begin with."

"When the prospectors came into South Pass, we lost land that was supposed to be ours by treaty," Tom said. "They are the ones that squatted on it. For that whole area, down the mountains to Lander, we got almost nothing. This used to be Shoshone hunting grounds and we camped here in winter. The Comanches were part of us then, too, before they split and went south. Then a few years later the government tried to take all that land north of Big Wind River. I remember that. Farmers from Nebraska came to homestead and we lost most of that land, too. That woman Inez don't know what she's talking about. Everybody buys things in Lander. This town practically lives off the Indians. And as for buying booze, I know plenty of whites that have a drinking problem, too. Nobody's perfect."

"Most people talk about the faults of others in order to build themselves up," I said. Inez had done just that, I said. It made me angry, I said.

"We always teach in peyote meetings that we're all trying to lead a better life but everybody falls down sometime along the way, some more than others," was Tom's answer. "You just have to have patience and help them out of their troubles. But when the government steps in and there's nothing you can do about it, the trouble begins. I could tell you stories about how the government kept saying they'd help us and then turned around and did just the opposite. After years and years, we finally got our judgment settled, the lawsuit against the government for placing the Arapahos on our reservation. The Arapaho all told me that they wanted their own reservation, too, but the government never gave them one. So they eventually sued and won a lawsuit for not getting the reservation the government had promised. But by that time the government said it had no more land to give them."

In the few days remaining for me at Wind River, Tom and I went to visit some more old-timers, the brothers Pete and Louie Aragon. "Those boys was darn good card players," said Tom. "Always tried to beat me, but I came back and beat them lots of times, too."

Pete and Louie and Tom talked about the stories their parents used to tell on long winter nights. Their mother was Shoshone, their father, Mexican.

"Coyote, he could talk to his hind end," Tom said.

"Coyote could do just about anything, more than any other person. He had supernatural power and he created us, too, the old people used to say," said Pete. "That's what my old people used to say. But that's all gone now. Kids, they just watch television."

"Like my grandson who's staying at my place now," Tom said.

There was going to be another peyote meeting Saturday night, just before I left Wind River. It was going to be among the Arapaho at Ethete, right next to Benny Goggle's place. Benny was the keeper of the sacred medicine wheel and one of the most important Arapaho elders. The meeting was hosted by Abraham Spotted Elk, a Northern Cheyenne married to one of Benny's daughters. The meeting was being put up by Abraham to honor his little daughter who had just gotten over a bad cold and was having her third birthday. Abraham was well known as an excellent singer.

We got to the meeting early, about four in the afternoon. The peyote teepee had been set up next to Benny's white frame house. Benny came outside and told us he wasn't going to the meeting but wanted to show us the medicine wheel. On one side of his house was a large painted wheel-like design, with different symbols painted on it—the medicine wheel.

The peyote meeting was an especially happy one because it celebrated the life of a child. At the beginning of the meeting Abraham presented her to the rest of the participants and said prayers for her. Tom was nearby, and he said a long prayer, too, as did Felix Groesbeck. After, the girl's mother took her into the house and put her to bed. The meeting ended the following morning when the little girl joined us to be with her father and mother at breakfast. It was also a farewell for me, and as people told me how much they liked me, I told my friends I appreciated everything they had done for me, all the blessings I received. I could never thank them enough.

A couple of days later, I loaded the trunk and back seat of my car, shook Tom's hand good-bye, and started on the long drive across the plains to the east, toward Iowa. The trip was almost a thousand miles and would take two days of steady driving. I followed U.S. Route 20 from the edge of the reservation a hundred miles or more to Casper, then drove on to Douglas, another half hour or so, for lunch. There was an old hotel in Douglas, the La Bonte, which was said to have good food. As I drove into town, I smiled at the giant statue of a Jackalope—a jackrabbit with a pair of antelope-like antlers—in the city square park. The old hotel was not far from the statue. It was right out of the old West. The lobby hadn't changed a bit over the years and I had a good hamburger steak and mashed potatoes in its restaurant.

I thought how much Tom would like the food and how much I'd enjoy having lunch with him.

I thought about Tom all the way to Lusk, the town where I planned to spend the night. The older generation of anthropologists was mostly interested in stories and recollections of the oldest Indian people who had good memories of life before the treaties were made and of the near-extinction of the buffalo. The older anthropologists wanted to preserve the past. Many of the Shoshone and Arapaho I knew also collected their folklore and stories, putting them down on tape sometimes. They also recorded songs from Sun Dances and learned other ceremonies from recordings. They were doing things that I had never expected, like becoming the curators of their own culture.

What *had* I learned from Tom and his friends? Both the Shoshone and Arapaho tribes had a strong sense of community. These tribes had been changing the rough outlines and composition of their people for generations, but there was always a core of tradition, tales, and beliefs that held people together. For Shoshone, there was the belief in *Dam Apë*, Our Father. He was prayed to at all ceremonies, Sun Dances, sweat lodges, and, of course, peyote meetings. Participation in these ceremonies conferred blessings on the people that took part in them. And why shouldn't they? Blessings and a sense of security and knowing who you were because others knew you were what community was all about. These rituals held people together and set the moral tone for all who participated in them. First and foremost was the idea of respect for all people regardless of background, regardless of tribe or race. Those values seemed to be in line with what I heard about how the First Nations on the east coast, in Virginia and Massachusetts, welcomed the English until they became aware that the English only wanted to take their land. The story of colonization soon became one of perpetual war between native peoples and European invaders. Over and over again, native nations and peoples tried to be treated as equals with the invaders, but time and time again they were ignored or rebuffed, treated as less than human.

I had been amazed and delighted that the Shoshone and Arapaho people had welcomed me and let me participate in the most personal and sacred side of their way of life, a way of life that kept the old values. I felt a warm glow of acceptance in every sweat ceremony or peyote meeting. A large part of this was due to Tom Wesaw's presence and the way he had accepted me, but I knew that I had gone half-way in meeting them, as they had me. I sensed that some of the best friends and best memories of my life were those of these past months in Wyoming.

On the east edge of Lusk, I stopped at a small motel that had individual cabins. When the proprietor answered his wall-mounted phone, I half-expected him to say, "I'll be there as soon as I can."

The next morning I drove across Nebraska on Highway 20, with a stop at Fort Robinson, an old army fort that had been turned into a state park. Crazy Horse had surrendered there. I stayed in one of the old barracks and it was easy to imagine the troops drilling on the parade grounds nearby. On to Crawford and Chadron, and Gordon, a town that had a long history of tension between whites and Sioux, who live just to the north on the Pine Ridge reservation in South Dakota. The Shoshone had been somewhat luckier than the Sioux—not as many wars, a better reservation. But, still, a conquered people.

I thought more about Tom Wesaw. Over and over I had noticed how his strength and service to the Shoshone people at Wind River came from the community and how important it was to be a part of the web of kinship that made up that community. Security and strength came from being a part of it. There was never any question that when people needed him, Tom would be there. People like Joe Lafferty, Tom's card-playing friend who died alone, were outside that web of kinship and the support it gave. In their social isolation they had almost no one they could depend upon when times were rough, but I could see that Tom's ministry extended to Joe, too. Tom had a remarkable ability to be inclusive, to see the humanness of every person regardless of background. That was why he was constantly urging the Shoshone to include everybody they could in the tribe, people of every kind of background, every ethnic or tribal or religious background. His was a multicultural ministry before the term had been invented.

Tom's community also existed for other reasons. It met during peyote meetings and sweats and during a host of other activities, from Shoshone Indian Days and the Sun Dance in the summer to dances and council meetings. Important questions dealing with enrollment and other business could be discussed over and over. Eventually, the people would find solutions. It was the essence of what is often called "grass-roots democracy," something that is rare indeed in modern America.

The fields of western Nebraska soon yielded to the rolling and almost empty Sand Hills of Cherry County, famous for its huge expanse of miles of rich grassland and herds of beef cattle. My stay with Tom occurred just before the beginning of the Red Power movement that began with the Sioux and the occupation of Wounded Knee, South Dakota, in the early 1970s. The Shoshone I knew at Wind River had been working to improve their tribe ever since they got the reservation by treaty in 1868. Red Power was nothing new to them; they had been working to change things for the better for many years. The Shoshone tribe was small enough so the voices of every faction could be heard in council meetings and in endless discussion after peyote meetings and sweats. It was like what the ideal form of democracy might be. The general council of the whole tribe held the decision-making power and anybody had the right to be heard. Things might not be ironed out now but in due time they would be.

I crossed Cherry County and drove across the fertile fields of eastern Nebraska toward the tidy farms of Iowa that presented a Grant Wood picture of peace and prosperity. I thought about how it was that people usually made the best decisions if they were only allowed to do so, and given the time and resources to do so. Only when powerful interests thwarted those decisions or when distant forces far removed from understanding the needs of the people prevailed, were those decisions wrong-headed.

I never saw Tom again. By the time I came back to Wind River, he had died while on a visit to his granddaughter Loreena in Montana. In the years after my stay with Tom, the United States has attempted to correct some of the unresolved problems that Tom showed me. In 1978, Congress ratified the American Indian Religious Freedom Act. This extends the guarantee of complete freedom of religion to all First Nations people. It means that using, possessing, or transporting peyote for religious purposes is no longer considered a crime. The important issue of heirship of Indian trust land remains in the news. In 1996 Eloise Cobell, a lawyer and member of the Blackfeet Nation of Montana, filed a class action suit against the United States for billions of dollars of unpaid leases on Indian trust land. The suit, Cobell v. Salazar, was finally settled in late 2009 and involves up to five hundred thousand tribal members across the United States. The settlement is for $3.4 billion, $1.4 billion of which will be given to plaintiffs and the remaining $2 billion to pay for voluntary buy-back and consolidation of fractionated land interests. The Wind River Shoshone and Arapaho filed a similar suit in 1979 and received $33.2 million in the summer of 2009. While the settlement did not go as far as Eloise Cobell wished, she stated that she was happy to receive the amount and was glad that Attorney General Holder approved what was long overdue.

The Shoshone tribe has reached a much more just resolution of tribal enrollment issues. Because of a decision allowing anyone of one-eighth Shoshone ancestry to join the tribe, hundreds of people applied for tribal membership. Enrollment went up and it followed that the per capita payments went down. When the Eastern Shoshone claimed that the new enrollees should be removed from the tribal rolls, a suit was filed to reinstate them. Eventually, that suit was thrown out and a more reasonable solution emerged in 1993. The Eastern Shoshone now enroll anyone who has at least one parent who is an enrolled Eastern Shoshone and has any

American Indian ancestry from both parents that adds up to one-quarter. Indian ancestry must be documented and a person can be enrolled at any point in his or her life. For example, if the mother is Eastern Shoshone and the father Arapaho, their child is eligible for enrollment in either tribe. The parents choose which one to enroll in.

As of 2009, Eastern Shoshone enrollment was 3,994, almost double what it was when I lived with Tom in 1969. However, enrollment is still controversial. The general council must approve all enrollments passed by the business council and some of these were still waiting in 2009 to be approved because a quorum of 250 tribal members is needed to hold a meeting.

Over the past forty years, American Indian religions, along with those originating in Asia, have been borrowed by practitioners outside of those societies. Collectively, these borrowed religious experiences have been labeled "New Age," indicating that they present a more relevant religious experience that goes beyond the traditions of the West. Lifted out of their cultural and community context, they do not confer the same spiritual beliefs as those within the culture, particularly when paid for. These derivative religious experiences include several religious practices described in this book. Tom Wesaw would have been appalled by attempts to take the religious practices of his people and graft them onto another culture. He would have encouraged people, as he did me, to understand these ceremonies, but without the proper context, much is lost in translation. Belief and practice take place within a tradition and a community that knows and accepts those beliefs and traditions. Removed from their social context and meaning, they become a spectacle and a commodity.

GLOSSARY

Allotment. See Dawes Act.

BIA. Abbreviation for the Bureau of Indian Affairs, a division of the United States Department of the Interior that administers the reservations of recognized Indian tribes.

Crowheart Butte. A prominent butte on the north side of the Wind River named after a battle in the 1850s in which the Shoshone leader Washakie defeated the Crow Indians. Tradition has it that he speared the heart of a Crow warrior.

Dawes Act. The Dawes or Severalty Act of 1887 was an important piece of legislation that gave each American Indian a certain amount of land to be held in trust; these were known as allotments. Misguided advocates of this act believed it was possible for Indians to become farmers and ranchers after about twenty years. However, unallotted reservation land could be sold to non-Indians, and after twenty years or so, Indians were also allowed to sell their allotments. About one-third of all reservation land was lost during this period until the act was finally repealed more than forty years later.

Eastern Shoshone. The Eastern Shoshone are the Wyoming Shoshone, the most eastern group of Shoshone Indians, who were placed on reservations in Idaho, Utah, and Nevada by treaties with the United States.

Fort Hall. An Indian reservation north of Pocatello, Idaho, and home to the Shoshone-Bannock. Established as a Hudson's Bay fur trading post in the 1830s, Fort Hall later was bought by American traders. It was never a military fort.

Fry bread. A delicious and staple food item among American Indians, fry bread is made from flour and baking powder or yeast and fried in hot oil.

Medicine Man. An Anglo-American name given to American Indian doctors; the Shoshone do not employ it. A traditional healer is a doctor or, in the Shoshone language, *bohugunt*.

Native American Church. A pan-tribal religious movement that originated among tribes in Oklahoma in the 1870s.

Northern Arapaho. The Northern Arapaho are those Arapaho Indians who became separated from their southern brothers during the period of warfare and treaty-making in the 1860s and 1870s. The Northern Arapaho were placed on the Shoshone or Wind River reservation by the United States in 1878 and the southern Arapaho were given a reservation with the southern group of Cheyenne in Oklahoma.

Per capita. A per capita is an equally divided amount of the total revenue of the Wind River reservation that is given to each enrolled Shoshone and Arapaho, usually monthly. Recent Shoshone per capitas have been about $250 per month, mostly from the sale of oil and natural gas. Arapaho per capitas are much smaller today, because the assets of the reservation are divided equally between the two tribes, and the Arapaho population is about twice that of the Shoshone.

Peyote box. A small box, long and narrow, that is often decorated and holds the owner's peyote staff and feathers used for blessing.

Peyote meetings. Peyote is a small green cactus that contains mescaline. It has been used as a sacrament by the Native American Church since it spread from Mexico to Oklahoma about 1870 and from there throughout the West. Ritual includes all-night services with songs, blessings, and prayers. It stresses reconciliation between tribes and with non-Indians and forbids the use of alcohol.

Sun Dance. The Sun Dance, called Standing in Thirst, or *Dago Wunere* in Shoshone, is a very old ritual with several variants found among many Plains and Intermountain tribes to the present. Performed in the summer, it stresses fasting without food or water for three days, dancing in a temporary lodge, and prayers and blessings. Today, its

emphasis is on tribal unity and healing.

Sun Dance whistle. Made from the hollow wing-bone of an eagle, the whistle is blown continuously by dancers as they dance in the Shoshone Sun Dance and has sacred value.

Sweat ceremonies. In aboriginal times, most American Indians had a small sweat lodge that was used for healing purposes and involved songs, blessings, and prayers. Those rituals continue to the present.

Treaty of 1868. The United States made a treaty with the Wyoming Shoshone in July of 1868. The treaty established the Wind River reservation in west-central Wyoming for the Eastern Shoshone.

Trout Creek. A creek flowing from the Wind River Range and the surrounding irrigated valley, the location of a number of Shoshone homesteads. The Wesaw family lives in this valley. A road winds up the valley from U.S. Highway 287, eventually leading into the mountains.

Tunison judgment. Named after George Tunison, an Omaha, Nebraska, attorney. Following an Act of Congress in 1913, he was hired by the Eastern Shoshone to sue the United States for illegally placing the Northern Arapaho on their reservation. The suit settled in 1938: the Shoshone received several million dollars from the United States but had to agree to divide the assets of the reservation in half with the Northern Arapaho.